A Practical Guide to Surrogacy

First print edition, September 2015 ISBN: 978-0-9846757-9-1

This book is not intended to provide legal advice or replace the counsel of an attorney, a physician, or any government or regulatory body. This information is provided purely as a guide to assist U.S. intended parents in navigating the surrogacy process in Mexico. We recommend intended parents familiarize themselves with the latest laws for their home countries and consult lawyers in both the U.S. and Mexico. It's also wise to confer with a physician prior to moving forward with any medical procedures.

Credits

Graphic design and artwork: Paul Daniels
Editor: Mangione, Payne & Associates
Contributors: Karla Dias, Anna-Lena Seip-Lächele, and Cristina Valdez

For my husband
Paul

Our children
Cody, Bryce, Gabriella, and Emma

And intended parents and surrogates around the world,
Including those who have completed their journey and those who are just
starting out

Contents

Acknowledgements

Our journey to expand our family from four to six took more than ten years, as we explored fertility treatments, adoption, and finally surrogacy. Many people helped us with specific aspects of the surrogacy process, and many others provided emotional support throughout the process. My husband Paul and I want to thank all of them. In particular we want to acknowledge and express our gratitude to the people who played a special role in making our journey a successful and, ultimately, a joyful one.

We are enormously grateful to our family and friends who supported our decision and now share our joy.

We feel especially blessed to have met Karla Dias, the woman who gave us the gift of carrying our babies, as well as her fiancé Ian, who was also our translator, and Karla and Ian's beautiful daughter.

We extend a special thank you to other parents through surrogacy: Marie, Stephan, Rhyannon, Mari, Lucas, Greg, Paul, Dania, Jens, Tess, Mark, Chad, and the countless others who continue to give back by providing updates on changing experiences and processes.

We want to thank the Mexican specialists with whom we worked during our journey and who continue to provide guidance. First, we want to thank Dr. Edgar Medina, Karla Gonzalez, and Oscar Valle of Imer IVF Fertility Clinic in Tijuana. They did an outstanding job assisting us through IVF, explaining everything and being patient when we were lost in Tecate. Their excellent work and care led to the creation of our two beautiful daughters. Second, we want to express our gratitude to Cristina Valdez of La Cigüeña del Bebé for providing expert legal advice, ensuring our contracts were in order, and sticking with us for more than a year of difficult processing with the U.S. Department of State. "Aunt" Cristina has been a blessing from the first day we met and we are extremely fond of her. She has provided the countless intended parents (IPs) we referred to her with support and guidance for a successful exit. Third, we want to express our appreciation to Dr. Adrian Flores of Insemer for his amazing delivery, medical services, and courage to do what is best for his patients. Our surrogate and daughters went through the pregnancy with no issues thanks to his expert care. Our family doctor verified that Dr. Flores' care not only matched the quality delivered in the U.S., but went beyond in ensuring that the serious medical conditions that arose never put our surrogate or our daughters in danger. His frank, can-do attitude and ethical treatment of his patients really helped set our journey in the right direction. Dr. Flores was truly one of the greatest blessings for our family.

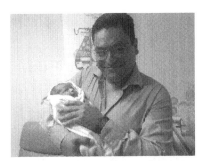

Dr. Flores holding one of our daughters

A special thank you to strangers we met who helped us during our extended stay in Mexico. To Chris and Les Parkin for your help in Merida with doctors' visits, a special Mother's day, and countless other days you helped us. To Sonya and Jeff of Casa Solana, and Sherri in Merida. To Viviana, Bertha, and Alma in Hermosillo. To the angel who held our daughter during the long flight from Merida to Tijuana because our 16-year-old son was not old enough. I don't know what I would have done had you not come along and selflessly offered your assistance.

Thank you also to people in the U.S. for making a difference. To Anna from John McCain's office and Katie from Jeff Flake's office for advocating for change. To Mr. Wallis and Mr. Adler for helping to change the citizenship and immigration process and their understanding of surrogacy in Mexico within the Department of State.

Finally, my husband and I want to thank our family for their love and support over the years. To our sons – Cody and Bryce – thank you for being amazing brothers not just to your two little sisters but to the countless other children we have opened our home to over the years trying to adopt. We are proud of the young men you have both become and how well you treat your sisters. A special thank you to our exchange sons, Jonathan and Jason, and their amazing parents.

Most of all thanks to God for sending us on this crazy journey and blessing us with two beautiful daughters after a ten-year wait.

Emma & Gabriella
born April 08, 2014
Villahermosa, Mexico

Foreword

Infertility can be an emotionally and mentally exhausting journey. Our journey was full of twists and turns. At times it can be hard to navigate the waters because the lack of international regulation with respect to surrogacy means that there are few rules that prevent profiteers from taking advantage of unsuspecting surrogates, intended parents, and the poor babies. We wrote this book to assist other IPs who are considering going abroad to Mexico or other countries for a part of or all of their surrogacy journey.

An official for American Citizen Services (ACS) in Merida told Paul and me that we were the first known American couple to work with the Department of State to complete the surrogacy process in Mexico. At the time, there was no established process and little knowledge of Mexican surrogacy laws. As a result, we underwent intense scrutiny. It took us more than a year and two months to finally reunite our four children and return to our home in the U.S. We had to travel to four U.S. consulates — Merida, Mexico City, Tijuana, and Nogales — and live in five cities in Mexico — Villahermosa, Merida, Mexico City, Tijuana, and Hermosillo —during the course of our journey. Although it was extremely difficult, we truly believe that we were sent on this journey to help others.

At the time of our journey, there was no U.S. government website that provided advice, nor was there a clear process for obtaining citizenship for our children through the Department of State. There was much confusion over the relevancy of The Hague Convention on Intercountry Adoption. We spent quite a bit of time and money trying to gain clarity. There was a chasm between the mature market the agencies painted in their advertisements and the reality of what was clearly a nascent market in Mexico.

We documented the entire process to prove that we followed not only the laws of Mexico but also those of the U.S. We started our blog, Surrogacy in Mexico: Debunking Facts from Fiction, while we were in Mexico. We had two goals in mind: To get assistance from the U.S. government to uphold our rights as citizens and to educate other IPs on the reality of surrogacy in Mexico. During our time in Mexico, we were fortunate to meet many wonderful IPs who have embarked upon the journey to Mexico to achieve their dreams of a family. We feel blessed by the support that this community has given us while we endured what was a surreal hardship for our family.

We are proud to know that U.S. laws regulating surrogacy were changed in October 2014, and they are now more favorable. Although the changes did not specifically affect our case, we do believe that our efforts to inform the U.S. Congress, leadership at the Office of Children's Issues of the Department of State, the U.S. Customs and Immigration Services (USCIS), U.S. Attorney General's office, and the White House helped improve the process in Mexico. Many positive changes have been implemented:

- Surrogacy cases are now processed in Mexico City where the staff has had more training and experience, and can collect DNA samples.
- Formula and diapers are now allowed at U.S. embassies and consulates across Mexico.[1]
- Department of State has posted a website with the exact instructions for the citizenship and exit process.[2]
- The process for DNA testing, interviewing, and obtaining the Consular Report of Birth Abroad has been streamlined.
- Both gestational (birth) and biological mothers can pass on citizenship as of October 2014.

We feel fortunate that we were able to make a difference in some small way. We are also pleased that the Department of State created a website for obtaining citizenship for children born through artificial reproductive technology (ART)[3] and surrogacy in Mexico, and that it incorporates the process and recommendations we provided during our numerous communications to various government officials.

---

[1] Security procedures at the embassy prohibited us from bringing a diaper bag into the office.

[2] http://mexico.usembassy.gov/eng/citizen_services/passports-birth-report/surrogacy-art-and-dna-testing.html

[3] http://www.mintzimmigrationlaw.com/2014/10/29/u-s-immigration-policy-catches-up-with-assisted-reproductive-technology/.

We are thankful for the support from the offices of Senator John McCain, Senator Jeff Flake, and Congressman Matt Salmon for helping remove the many obstacles before us so we could finally bring our daughters home. We are also extremely thankful to Rosa Urquiola and Elizabeth Range of USCIS for providing us with an alternative route for resolution via humanitarian parole.

Although the process has come a long way, quite a bit more is still needed before the market is truly mature. Because surrogacy is unregulated in general, many agencies have sprung up to capitalize on the hopes and dreams of unsuspecting IPs and poor surrogate mothers.

Our experience with our surrogate, the Mexican doctors, agencies, and government was very pleasant. We believe that if others follow the process we outline in this book, they will have a less stressful and less risky journey to surrogacy in Mexico. Like the officials in the Mexican federal government and Tabasco state government, we are concerned that the greedy few who have been the center of documentaries and news clips will ruin the opportunity for other parents and surrogates to experience the joy and beauty that surrogacy can offer. We hope that this guide will help IPs cut through the clutter of misinformation to focus on what matters most to the families created through surrogacy.

Jeanne Daniels, September 2015

A Surrogate's Perspective

Being a surrogate mother is one of the most gratifying things a woman can do. It's also one of the hardest. Even though the babies you carry are not yours — they don't belong to you — they will always be a part of you. You will always keep them in your mind.

I won't pretend that saying goodbye to the babies is easy. It's not as difficult, however, when you have peace of mind. I will always thank God for letting Jeanne and I meet. She understands that surrogate mothers have worries and doubts. She knows that we wonder what kind of future lies ahead for these tiny persons we carry. We worry about the risks they might face.

If you're thinking about becoming a surrogate, ask yourself this question: Would you be able to give a baby away? A baby you carried in your womb? A baby that you felt moving and kicking? A baby that you are as responsible for bringing into this world as the parents?

And would you be able to do this without knowing what will happen to this child? I think most surrogates would answer no to the last question — or at least admit that it would be incredibly difficult.

That answer doesn't mean that a surrogate wants to be a second mother for the child. No. As mothers ourselves, we surrogates understand why the intended parents may be concerned about this. We make this sacrifice of our bodies and lives to help others feel the joy that we have felt of being a parent. It is our heart's journey to help others. I want parents to understand that surrogates will have a peace of mind by being able to take on the role of an aunt or of a friend of the family. Someone who sometimes wants to catch up to see how the parents and babies are doing. Knowing that our sacrifice truly made a difference for the parents and the little persons we carry can bring peace of mind to a surrogate when it comes time to present our gift to you.

For me personally, the idea of a long-term relationship was one of the things that helped me make the decision to embark on this journey. Jeanne is a really caring person and fully understands why our relationship is a showcase for a successful surrogacy journey. We didn't just talk. We conversed. We didn't just meet. We got to know each other. As a result, we learned how much alike we are. I got to know her family, what they do for living, their beliefs, and how the babies would fit into their lives. As a result, I'm sure these babies are growing up in a great family full of love and blessings. The relationship we developed helped dissipate the doubts and worries I had, and left me with a feeling of happiness. We make a point to get our families together at least once a year and talk about once a month. Our daughter and their children are close – like extended families. For us, we not only helped a family realize its dreams but extended our own.

To me, it's important for parents to know that this type of relationship is possible. Don't fear that we will try to take your place. Understand that you can build a friendship that, for the surrogate, means she won't ever have to worry about what happened to this child — this beautiful gift from God. It means she will never have to say goodbye. And for the parents, it's a way of giving a gift back to the person who helped you make your dream of having a child come true.

Karla Dias, September 2015

Another Parent's Perspective

As a parent through surrogacy in Mexico myself and a admin/committee team member of Families through Surrogacy UK/Europe, I can only say thank you to Jeanne for all her time, effort, and information. Embarking on a surrogacy journey can be overwhelming. It is hard to know what information is correct and can be trusted.

I admire Jeanne's strong spirit and desire to help others. Over the course of my journey, we became friends. By sharing the process and details of her journey and providing guidance along the way, Jeanne taught me not to give up hope. From her I learned that you can fulfill your dreams.

Our daughter was born in Villahermosa, Mexico, in June 2015. Without Jeanne's help, our angel would not exist. I could not imagine the world without this adorable baby in it. We love her so much!

Jeanne not only has knowledge about surrogacy in Mexico but also about surrogacy in other countries. Through her work, Jeanne has helped so many misinformed intended parents.

I was impressed that she sought out other intended parents who are actively involved to understand the many challenges and the most effective solutions. Jeanne often reached out to me after my experience to gain insights and understand the changes in surrogacy in Mexico. Together we are a great team, building a community based on sharing the information with others for future parents to stay up to date.

To all intended parents out there, whether your surrogate is already pregnant or whether you are considering surrogacy as an option: Don´t give up. It can be done. Our beautiful daughter is proof! I wish you all the luck in the world!

Anna-Lena Seip-Lächele, Germany, September 2015

Introduction

Perception is not always reality for those embarking on the journey to parenthood. The road is often filled with twists, turns, and, in many cases, heartache. When you decide to have children — whether it's your first child or your fifth — you need a strong foundation to build on. The journey can take a toll on the travelers, especially when genetic, biological, or physical factors prevent a couple from conceiving and carrying a baby to full term. These factors affects not only heterosexual couples but also same-sex couples. Adoption works well for many, but it isn't for everyone.

I have written this book because my husband Paul and I attempted to expand our family over a period of ten years. Our efforts resulted in many difficult and painful situations, so we explored other options. Ultimately, we decided that surrogacy was the best choice for our family. We investigated surrogacy in the U.S., India, Mexico, and Thailand. We were going to do the implantation in Mexico and surrogacy in the US. It just so happened though the surrogate we really wanted lived in Tijuana. We found peace of mind knowing that surrogacy in Mexico was altruistic instead of commercial, the cost was far less than in the U.S., the infant mortality rates were close to those of the U.S., and the medical care was just as good.

Based on our experience and that of other IPs we've interacted with over the past two years, we've found that regardless of the country of origin of the intended parents (IPs) or the location in which the surrogate resides, the players and the phases of the surrogacy process are similar. So, while this book focuses on IPs from the U.S. engaging with a surrogate in Mexico, much of it is applicable to IPs and surrogates from other countries.

Our goal for this book is to provide hope and help to those of you who may feel ready to throw in the towel after years of chasing down multiple avenues or those of you who are just starting on the journey of bringing children into your family. We hope that providing insight into our experience and sharing the lessons we learned will help you navigate the surrogacy process in Mexico and bring your new baby (or babies) home as quickly as possible.

Whether you are just beginning your journey or have been traveling this bumpy road for a while, have patience. Don't give up or fret. When the time is right for you, it will happen. And, as you read this book, don't become overwhelmed or frustrated, and don't lose hope. As difficult as our journey was, we would do it all again. Why? Because today, we're fulfilling our dream of a lifetime of the laughter, the joy, and the aggravation that comes with children. What more could we ask for in life?

Why Read This Book?

This book provides insights, prescriptive guidance, and suggestions to help you determine if surrogacy is right for you and, if so, to help you navigate the surrogacy process. Only you and your family know what you can afford financially, physically, and emotionally. Surrogacy should be undertaken only after careful consideration and with a full understanding of what can go right and what can go wrong.

The issue with surrogacy is that having a child is such an emotionally intimate experience. Consequently, people often make decisions using their emotions or *affective domain* instead of thinking through all the considerations logically before making a decision. With surrogacy, you may find yourself in a really difficult position requiring you to make decisions that are emotionally taxing. There are so many questions that run through your mind. Sometimes your desire for a baby is so strong that you end up believing — or talking yourself out of doubting — information that is incorrect.

Unfortunately, surrogacy is still a somewhat unregulated market. The laws vary from country to country and there is often a heated debate over whether it should be allowed. Because oversight is limited (even nonexistent in some places), the industry is riddled with profiteers trying to make a fast buck at the expense of IPs and surrogates.

Whether your surrogacy takes place in the U.S., Mexico, India, Thailand, or another country, at the end of the day it is *your* journey. Many of the sites, agencies, and individuals we researched and interacted with proved to be masters of fiction. If you aren't the captain of your own ship throughout the journey, agencies or individuals may steer you in the wrong direction.

Our hope is that you can learn from our mistakes, benefit from our successes, and complete the process more logically. The information provided in this book is based on our personal experience as well as input from dozens of other IPs who visited our website to read our blog posts and reference the process we documented. Many of them shared their stories with us.

This guide not only describes our journey but also provides checklists we created, adjusted, and updated along the way. Many of the agency checklists we received were incomplete or skewed to favor the agency's agenda. One agency, for example, sent us a checklist that was so riddled with errors that, had we followed it, we would have wasted a lot of time and money.

For example, the checklist indicated we had to get a DNA test from an AABB accredited lab. The list the agency provided included names of labs in Mexico, each of which charged approximately $4,000[4] per test. The truth is that only AABB accredited labs *in the U.S.* are accepted. Fortunately, we learned that bit of information before we wasted money on a lab in Mexico.

An accurate, complete checklist helps IPs avoid extra expenses and aggravation.

Our Journey

Every surrogacy journey is unique. Ours led us down a long road filled with complications and unforeseen circumstances that at times made it hard to follow. If asked, we would definitely do it all over again, as our daughters are amazing. What has been frustrating is the number of agencies that have used our case for their own benefit. There are some that say we experienced complications because we didn't use a US agency. In fact, we started with a US Agency. In the end we used 2 reputable Mexican agencies and self managed the surrogate to insure the process was altruistic.

The best agencies we found were in Mexico because they knew the laws, processes, and language. We started with an agency based in the U.S. but quickly found that to be a big mistake. That US agency scheduled an appointment for us with an *in vitro fertilization* (IVF) clinic called Imer, which is located in Tijuana. We began the procedure to prepare for our journey, and we found the Imer doctors and staff to be highly professional. It was the staff at

---

[4] Unless otherwise stated, we use U.S. dollars as the currency.

3

Imer that alerted us to the fact that the U.S. agency had given us incorrect information that could have gotten us into legal trouble in Mexico. We learned that the agency was engaging in unethical business practices that included advertising procedures that are illegal in Mexico such as embryo adoption and failing to deliver promised services. We continued to work with Imer, but we fired the U.S. agency.

We then hired La Cigüeña del Bebé, a Mexican agency that provides legal process services, and Insemer, an agency that provides delivery services. We worked directly with our surrogate and arranged travel and lodging on our own. This turned out to be the best thing we could have done. This approach gave us more control over our funds and costs, and more flexibility in choosing various providers.

Figure 1 summarizes the path we took in engaging agencies and other providers.

Figure 1. Jeanne and Paul's Path to Self Management

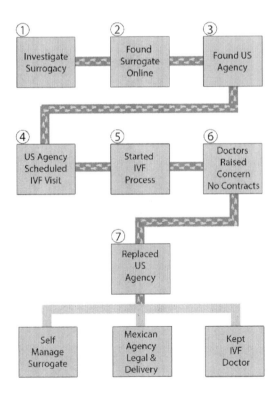

We learned that none of the agencies had all the answers or knew the entire process. We documented what we learned along the way. The process with Mexico was great in the end. We had no major roadblocks with the Mexican government. It wasn't until we started the citizenship and immigration process with the U.S. government that we ran into issues. The problems arose due to the fact that the processes and documentation involved were still nascent.

We found that Imer, the IVF clinic in Tijuana, had great first-time success rates for fresh embryo implantations. We liked the fact that they were close to where our surrogate lived and only a five-hour drive from our home. Originally we had planed to have our baby born in San Diego – just 20 minutes over the border. Our surrogate and her family members had all applied for US Visas – so she could have the baby in the US and it would be close by. The US agency had assured us this would not be a problem. It was the Mexican doctors that warned us it could take longer than we think for our surrogate to get her visa – so we better insure we honored Mexican laws and had a back up plan in case she did not receive her visa in time. The US agency was not forthcoming with the contracts or Mexican agreements and our doctors warned us that if we did not have a legal contract in Mexico – they would not do the implantation.

Unfortunately, we found ourselves in a bit of a bind. We had already started the medication process prepare our surrogate's womb and collect genetic material. Karla and her fiancé helped us investigate other service providers in Mexico — Insemer for delivery services and La Cigüeña del Bebé for legal services. Both agencies agreed to work with us.

Insemer is in the business of reproduction as well surrogacy. Dr. Adrian Flores handles reproductive issues and delivers babies from all types of patients, not just surrogates. As a result, the staff is highly experienced not only in reproductive issues but also in treating complications such as anemia. No matter what time of day we called or what issues or concerns we expressed, Insemer either had the answer right away or put us in touch with someone who could help us.

5

The people at Insemer were brutally honest. They had our best interest at heart, not their own. We were impressed with the honesty and integrity we experienced with Dr. Flores and his staff. Although he had a relationship with the agency we were initially using, Dr. Flores made it clear that proceeding without a contract would have all of us (IPs and surrogate) in trouble with the Mexican government. His counsel in this area demonstrated that he was committed to giving everyone involved in the surrogacy the information needed to make an informed decision.

At first, we were interested in an embryo adoption to avoid a genetic heart defect my husband has. The American agency advertised this as a viable option. However, we learned from Cristina Valdez, the attorney from La Cigüeña del Bebé, and Dr. Medina, the IVF doctor in Tijuana, that this is illegal and they would not work with us if we chose embryo adoption. They were also honest with us and with Karla at the beginning to ensure the arrangement was truly altruistic in nature.

We found we needed Insemer only for delivery services. During the contract discussions, Dr. Flores was adamant that we discuss the hard issues, not just the easy ones. Topics included our beliefs on abortion, how many tries we were willing to take (not just us but the surrogate), what the birth plan would be for a singleton, twins, and so forth. He also clearly explained that there is no guarantee a baby will result, and that we needed to be prepared for a variety of complications along the way.

From the beginning, both the IVF and delivery doctors were careful to ensure that my husband and I were on the same page as the surrogate to eliminate any stressful situations. These discussions were really useful because, for example, we found that our surrogate wanted a vaginal delivery. We all agreed to this for a singleton. However, before becoming pregnant, we had fully discussed the need for a C-section in the case of twins or if complications occurred.

Dr. Medina, Dr. Flores, and Cristina Valdez all had experience with surrogacy in Mexico and references from IPs from outside of Mexico who acted as trusted advisors to us to ensure a successful surrogacy. We found that the best advisors are people who have traveled the path before.

In summary, it turned out that that first U.S. agency's poor performance was a blessing in disguise. Instead of ending up the way some unsuspecting IPs have, we took charge of our own destiny. We handled our surrogacy journey in the same way we approach our business: with caution, lots of research, and the advice of experts in many different areas. The best thing we did was follow our own business acumen and instinct. Despite some unnecessary expenses, we were able to fulfill our dream of growing our family.

Understanding Surrogacy

Let's start with basics. There are two types of surrogates: *traditional surrogate* and *gestational substitute*.

- A **traditional surrogate** provides genetic material (the egg) to create the embryos, undergoes IVF, and carries the baby to term. In this case, the surrogate is not only the carrier but also the biological mother of the child.

- A **gestational substitute** carries the baby to term but has no biological connection to the child. The eggs come from the intended mother or from an egg donor.

In cases of embryo adoption, donated frozen embryos might be used. Embryos might be created from donated sperm and eggs when both IPs are infertile or when they do not wish to pass on life-threatening genetic anomalies.

Legal Implications

It's important to understand the legal implications of each type of surrogate. According to Mexican law, a child born through a gestational substitute is recognized as the IPs' legal child at the time of birth, whether or not the child is genetically connected to the IPs.

U.S. law, however, requires that IPs prove a genetic link before they can obtain U.S. citizenship for the child. If there is no genetic link, then the child must be adopted. The problem is, U.S. couples are not permitted to adopt Mexican children under five years of age without filing exceptions with The Hague Convention as well as the U.S. and Mexican governments. IPs could end up stranded in Mexico for years trying to sort out what to do. Consequently, IPs working with a surrogate in Mexico should avoid embryo adoption and ensure a genetic link to the child by providing the egg(s) or sperm or both.

In addition to Mexican and U.S. laws, surrogacy arrangements in both countries (as well as in 73 other countries) are affected to some degree by the Hague Convention on Intercountry Adoption.[5] This agreement provides guidelines and

---

[5] For details on the Hague Convention Adoption Treaty, visit http://adoption.about.com/od/international/f/whathague.htm.

procedures for adoption across international borders. It can complicate surrogacy arrangements when its provisions clash with domestic surrogacy laws and parental rights.

The Hague Convention is working on guidelines and procedures to regulate surrogacy. One of our sources (a legal advisor to the U.S. officials helping to draft the surrogacy guidelines) indicated that it will take years to finalize and execute the guidelines.

In Tabasco, Mexico, the law governing surrogacy distinguishes between traditional surrogacy and gestational substitute. With traditional surrogacy, IPs must adopt the baby and the surrogate must relinquish her claim to her biological connection. Gestational substitute agreements, however, list the IPs as the legal parents of the child and do not require adoption.

Because we were one of the first couples to request U.S. citizenship for children born of surrogacy in Mexico with U.S. IPs, the differences between traditional surrogacy and gestational substitute were not well understood. As a result, obtaining U.S. citizenship for one of our daughters took more than a year.

As a result of our case, the U.S. embassy and consular offices now have a much better understanding of how to handle surrogacy cases in Mexico. The process is much more streamlined. However, complications are likely to occur if you choose traditional surrogacy and plan to deliver in Mexico.

Considerations when Going Abroad

Surrogacy in the U.S. can be risky for IPs because some state laws favor the surrogate and some states do not honor surrogacy contracts. If a surrogate decides to keep the baby, she can move to one of those states and state laws will permit her to do so. In some cases, IPs have had to pay child support even though they had to relinquish their baby to the surrogate.[6]

This section presents considerations IPs need to thoroughly understand with respect to the birth country. These considerations apply not only to IPs from the U.S., but also to those from Spain, Germany, France, and others.

Medical/Health Issues

Infant mortality rates and anemia are the two primary medical and health issues IPs need to consider. Medical training requirements and the cleanliness and quality of care at hospitals and clinics is another.

Infant Mortality

With respect to infant mortality, Mexico compares somewhat favorably with the U.S. Mexico is number 123 of the 224 countries ranked at https://www.cia.gov/.../the-world-.../rankorder/rawdata_2091.txt. This means it has the 123rd highest infant mortality rate in the world. The U.S. is 169th and India is 50th.

Anemia

Anemia rates during pregnancy are higher in developing countries such as Mexico, particularly in the case of multiples.[7] Anemia can be life threatening for the mother and the child, so it's important to correlate life-threatening probabilities such as anemia with infant mortality. One of the reasons we chose

---

[6] For details on other these types of cases, visit http://www.ivf.net/ivf/us-court-rules-that-surrogate-mother-can-keep-child-o3019.html, http://us103.com/surrogate-keeps-baby-would-be-parents-must-pay-785-monthly/, http://timesofindia.indiatimes.com/india/Baby-Manjis-case-throws-up-need-for-law-on-surrogacy/articleshow/3400842.cms, and http://unitesiblings.org/international-ivfsurrogacy-and-the-quest-for-basic-human-dignity-and-respect/.

[7] Source: http://www.ajtmh.org/content/77/1/44.full.

Mexico over India is that both the infant mortality rate and the rate of anemia among women in their childbearing years are significantly lower in Mexico.

Medical Training

The breadth and quality of legally mandated medical training for doctors, nurses, and other medical professionals are an important area of concern. As in the U.S., doctors in Mexico average 12 years of education. They must have a medical license to practice and must display their certifications.

Hospitals and Other Medical Facilities

Medical tourism is a growing industry in Mexico. As a result, hospitals and clinics are generally clean and well run. IPs should, however, check out the facilities recommended by the delivery doctor and choose one based on such factors as cleanliness, quality of care, and infant mortality rate.

Ask for a tour of the facility and interview the staff. When we did our investigation, we were not comfortable with the quality of care at one of the hospitals, but found Star Medica in Tabasco to be very impressive.

Language Proficiency

Communication is key to navigating the surrogacy process. If you're not fluent in Spanish, and medical personnel, hospital staff, and agency employees aren't fluent in English, you may not understand what's happening well enough to make sound decisions. Although the various entities have translators on staff, they are not always available when you need them. Also, these translators are employees or contractors of the agency or medical facility. If you are not fluent in Spanish, we recommend you hire a translator who works for you and focuses on what is in your best interest.

Human Factors

The health and well-being of the surrogate has a direct impact on the health and well-being of the child. As you talk to medical personnel and agency staff, make sure that they treat the surrogate with respect, dignity, and extreme care. A child's personality traits start developing after five months in the womb, so pay close attention to attitudes of anyone involved in the surrogacy process. That helps you avoid conditions that could have a negative impact on the emotional, psychological, and physical state of the surrogate and the child.

Legal and Regulatory Issues

The best way to avoid legal and/or regulatory Issues is to ensure you understand the laws of your country and the birth country. In other words, if you're going abroad for surrogacy, don't proceed without investigating the applicable laws and understanding what implications they can have on you, the surrogate, and your child(ren). You also have a responsibility to yourself to understand what it takes to stay within the laws of your home country.

Mexican Laws

Surrogacy is legal in the State of Tabasco because there are state laws governing surrogacy arrangements. The laws are subject to change at the end of 2015 so it is important that you make sure you understand them before proceeding. Many IPs select the city of Villahermosa as their surrogacy destination because of the good selection of private hospitals and rich culture.

There are also federal laws in Mexico that govern child trafficking. These include requirements for blood tests to detect sexually transmitted diseases (STDs) and attestations by IVF doctors regarding the creation of embryos. IVF clinics, for example, must be certified and certifications must be on display. Several couples have experienced longer and more complicated exit processes because they could not provide the required permit to prove the procedures were completed in compliance with Mexican Laws.

Unfortunately, we've run across individuals and agencies who attempt to circumvent these laws in various ways. One agency, for example, advertises the creation of embryos for HIV-infected parents in the U.S. or other countries. The agency ships the embryos to Mexico for implantation, which violates the requirement we were told from 2 Mexican IVF clinics that the IPs had to be STD free before they could legally do an implantation.[8]

---

[8] The same agency recently made the news in Mexico for mistreating and abandoning pregnant surrogates. Visit our Facebook page at https://www.facebook.com/pages/Surrogacy-In-Mexico-debunking-facts-from-fiction/385820588227450?fref=ts for articles on this topic.

Clean Bill of Health for the Child

Mexico will not issue a birth certificate or Mexican passport unless the IPs can produce a letter from a pediatrician confirming the health of the baby. This law ensures that medically fragile children are not put at risk by subjecting them to travel. In a highly publicized 2015 case, a Canadian couple had difficulty obtaining birth certificates because the babies were not ready to leave the hospital due to one having a brain bleed.[9] If the baby is not well enough to go for the interview, and state and federal authorities believe it is not in the child's best interest to be moved, they will not issue the documents needed to do so.

Impact of International Laws

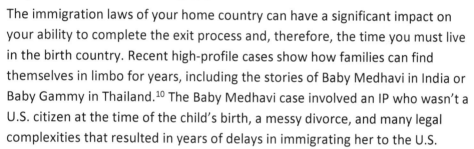

The immigration laws of your home country can have a significant impact on your ability to complete the exit process and, therefore, the time you must live in the birth country. Recent high-profile cases show how families can find themselves in limbo for years, including the stories of Baby Medhavi in India or Baby Gammy in Thailand.[10] The Baby Medhavi case involved an IP who wasn't a U.S. citizen at the time of the child's birth, a messy divorce, and many legal complexities that resulted in years of delays in immigrating her to the U.S.

In the Baby Gammy case, which made the news in 2014, the surrogate delivered twins, one of which had Down syndrome. The IPs, who are from Australia, took the healthy twin home and left the one with Down syndrome in Thailand with the surrogate. One reason leaving the baby home is that the Australian government has restrictions on granting citizenship to individuals with disabilities or genetic disorders. By the time the Australian government eased these restrictions, the surrogate had decided to keep the baby along with the funds that had been raised to support him. The point here is the laws of both Australia and Thailand complicated the situation and put the surrogate, the IPs, and the innocent child in a very messy situation.

---

9 http://www.cbc.ca/news/canada/british-columbia/greg-and-elaine-smith-fight-to-bring-surrogate-born-twins-home-from-mexico-1.2933862.

[10] http://unitesiblings.org/international-ivfsurrogacy-freedom-freedom-freedom/

While stories like this one make the news, other IPs have successfully brought their children home with only a few minor issues. The key is to avoid heartbreaks by understanding the laws, taking into account the maturity of the market, and avoiding the common mistakes that get IPs in trouble.

Distance and Travel Requirements

Depending on where you live, Mexico might seem like a long way from home. For U.S. citizens, however, it's much closer than India, and other countries where surrogacy is legal. Distance is an important consideration because you will need to travel to Mexico or India for key activities in the surrogacy process. You'll need to make at least three trips to:

- Investigation of hospitals, clinics, and doctors, taking lab tests, and meeting your surrogate
- Embryo creation
- Delivery and processing of paperwork to return to the U.S. with your child

You may need to make additional trips, some of which may be unexpected. In your planning, be sure to consider what you will do if you have to go early due to premature birth, and what you'll do if issues arise after delivery. Examples include health issues with the infant and roadblocks during the process of getting birth certificates or obtaining U.S. citizenship.

At the time of this book's publication, it takes 5-6 weeks for US Passport and Citizenship and two to four months to get a Mexican passport for a child born as a result of a surrogacy arrangement. We've talked to several couples from the U.S., Germany, Spain, and the Netherlands who took their children home using the passport of their respective countries and then obtained a Mexican passport at a Mexican embassy in their home country. Check with your facilitator or agency to find out current processing times for Mexican passports.

Although Mexico does not require a visa for U.S. citizens, the government does issue what is called a *tramite* when you are traveling to and from Mexico. The tramite tracks your air and sea travel. It is not used for land border crossings.

Mexican government officials may ask to see your tramite to prove you were in Mexico at the time you executed the contract with the surrogate and at the time the baby was delivered. It is wise to take a picture of the tramite with your phone so you have a copy with you if you need it. The tramite is good for six months. After six months, you must leave Mexico and return to have a new tramite issued. We lived in Mexico for nearly a year, so we became very familiar with the tramite process.

Political and Structural Stability

If you pay attention to the news in the U.S., you'll hear a lot of negative sound bites regarding crime, corruption, bribery, and substandard living conditions in Mexico. Our experience shows that the events that make the news are the exception, not the rule. The Mexican officials we worked with were highly professional and were concerned about protecting the children, the surrogate, and the IPs.

Altruistic versus Commercial Surrogacy

Mexican law is very clear on the difference between *commercial surrogacy* and *altruistic surrogacy*.

- In commercial surrogacy, the surrogate is permitted to earn a profit beyond the expenses of the pregnancy.

- In altruistic surrogacy, the surrogate cannot personally profit from carrying the child. IPs can, however, reimburse the surrogate for expenses related to carrying and giving birth to the child.

Commercial surrogacy arrangements specify payment at specific milestones: upon pregnancy, first trimester, second trimester, and delivery of the baby. Altruistic arrangements provide payment of expenses starting around the time of IVF and for up to one month after delivery.

While commercial surrogacy is legal in the U.S., it is illegal in Mexico. It is important that you take steps to ensure that your surrogacy agreement clearly specifies an altruistic arrangement.

Because we were one of the first known cases of surrogacy in Mexico, our case was reviewed extensively by both the U.S. and Mexican governments. Our experience made it clear that both governments expect proof that the arrangement is altruistic. If either government believes your arrangement is not altruistic, you'll likely face complications when you try to take the child home. You could even face issues related to child trafficking.

Beware, because some agencies try to work around the commercial-versus-altruistic surrogacy issue by paying an all-inclusive fee to a clinic and then having the clinic pass on what they claim is a donation to the surrogate. While this tactic has sometimes enabled them to circumvent current laws, it has raised concerns with the Mexican government. Officials who are working to reform the laws are trying to determine the best way to protect surrogates and ensure that only altruistic surrogacy is used.

Mexican laws are slated to change at the end of 2015. Be sure to stay up to date on any legal changes and understand the implications of your choices. That way you are less likely to get stuck in country when you try to take the baby home.[11]

Our Personal Insights into the IP/Surrogate Relationship

While some IPs have concerns about altruistic surrogacy, the altruistic nature of surrogacy in Mexico made us more comfortable for several reasons. Our opinion is that commercial surrogacy tends to keep IPs too far removed from the human side of the surrogate, her environment, and her health. Our surrogate not only made a major difference in our lives, but also we made a difference in hers.

While altruistic surrogacy seeks to prevent payments to the woman who carries your child, you're still able to give much to the person who is giving so much to you. The key is to make sure that the surrogacy arrangement is more than just a legal contract. Instead, develop a personal relationship between the two families.

In an altruistic arrangement, IPs pay reasonable expenses for the surrogate. But just what is "reasonable"? We recommend a holistic approach in figuring this

---

[11] Visit http://lilianamadrigal.mx/.../iniciativa-de-reforma-al-codig.../ for an article on proposed changes. This article is in Spanish. For an English translation, visit https://www.facebook.com/permalink.php?story_fbid=527966410679533&id=3858205 88227450

out. It is easier and better for both the surrogate and your family to pay an expense stipend, perhaps weekly or monthly, so that the surrogate has access to the money as she is incurring the expenses. Why is this really critical? If the surrogate doesn't have enough money to cover basic needs, there is a higher risk of developmental delays or miscarriage. Many surrogates have at least one child of their own. When a mother is forced to choose between feeding her child or herself, chances are she'll feed her child first. We opted not only to help Karla but also to provide for her daughter to ensure that both were getting proper nourishment and care. We did things like buy vitamins and calcium supplements for both to give her a peace of mind. This fostered a stress-free pregnancy. We're convinced that our pregnancy went as well as it did because of our close relationship with Karla and our desire to understand her needs.

While Karla's motives were altruistic, we are happy that she benefited from our relationship. She was able to stay home with her daughter. Her family was able to save for and purchase newer items such as a refrigerator, stove, dryer, table, and beds with the money they normally would have spent for Karla's everyday living expenses. Of the 13 surrogates we interviewed, we chose Karla because it was clear to us she was not motivated by money.

A strong relationship with your surrogate also gives you visibility into her environment so you can provide assistance that promotes a healthy pregnancy. We've heard of several cases where the agency said that the surrogate's living conditions were acceptable. The IPs, however, felt that there were elements in the environment that might pose health hazards to the surrogate, the fetus, and the surrogate's family. Consequently, they moved the surrogate and her family into a healthier, more comfortable environment.

In our case, Karla incurred some expenses that were not covered by the stipend, but were necessary. We paid them because it was the best thing for Karla. Early in the pregnancy, Karla and her family had the opportunity to move into a larger home. We were visiting to celebrate her daughter's third birthday and to see an ultrasound of our twins at the time she and Ian, her fiancé, did a walkthrough of the home. They invited us to join them.

Although the home was much more spacious than their current one, we saw several hazards that concerned us. There was no flooring in the living room or bedrooms, which presented a trip hazard. There was black mold on the shower doors in the bathroom, the shower walls were crumbling, and the toilet was cracked causing sewage to leak into the shower stall.

Despite these defects, the home had many advantages: two bedrooms instead of one and more living space for the same monthly rent. It was closer to their schools (Karla and Ian are both students), and to Karla's family. Karla and Ian were willing to make the repairs to have a bigger place for the same money. We respected their willingness to put in the labor to improve their living situation. We would have done the same thing in their case.

Although they didn't expect any help from us, we decided our experience in home improvement projects could benefit them. We've laid flooring in our own home and have done quite a few tile projects. We know where to go for affordable but quality flooring, tile, and bathroom fixtures. So it was natural for us to offer our help. Karla and Ian covered the cost of materials. We provided our labor as a "labor gift" for Karla so she could relax. We knew she would work hard carrying and delivering the babies, and we wanted to do something special.

Although it resulted in some expenses we hadn't planned on due to the additional travel to Tijuana, and the remodel weekend was a busy one, it was well worth the time and money. The experience of our two families working together helped bring us even closer.

Our relationship proved to be important throughout the pregnancy and after the delivery. When we hit major emergencies such as Karla's anemia, we trusted that what they were asking for was necessary. We were also just as concerned with the impact on Karla as we were for the health of our babies. We made decisions based on what was best for all, without any conflicts during what were very tense situations.

We drew strength from each other as we worked through a very new, scary process that was not thoroughly understood. We surprised the hospital staff when both families (including the babies) stayed together in the hospital. Karla and I were together every step of the way.

Ian was instrumental in providing translation services for us when we went to get the birth certificates. Karla and Ian were our witnesses for the birth certificates, which made the process easier with the Registro Civil. .

Our philosophy with respect to our relationship with Karla was one of ensuring peace of mind for us and comfort and safety for her. Nothing was negotiated up front in this area, but as IPs, we did take an assertive, responsible role in eliminating any situations that could lead to difficulties during the pregnancy or after, and to make the experience as pleasant as possible for everyone.

The U.S. agency we originally dealt with had worked with another couple whose surrogate miscarried. We couldn't help wondering if the agency was tuned into the surrogate's environment. We wondered if better monitoring of the surrogate's health and quality of life could have resulted in a better outcome.

We believe that our close relationship with Karla and her family resulted in a healthier pregnancy and also provided a better emotional and psychological experience for all of us.

When we started looking into surrogacy, we saw a documentary about a commercial surrogacy in India. The surrogate longed to know what type of life the child would have. The psychological toll this took on her saddened us. We wanted to make sure our situation was different and that our surrogate would feel confident that the children she carried would be well cared for.

Our relationship continues today. We keep in touch via Facebook, Skype, and phone. Karla, Ian, and their daughter have visited us in the U.S. and we've stayed at their home in Tijuana. We made a pact to get our families together at least once a year so our girls will know each other. We consider Karla and Ian to be an aunt and uncle to all four of our children.

Altruistic Surrogacy and Costs

We actually think an altruistic arrangement reduces unexpected costs and complications. We spoke to a Canadian couple that contracted with a commercial surrogate. The IPs paid her a fee to carry the babies and cover her expenses. They ended up paying again for a number of expenses because the surrogate spent the money they gave her on other items early in the pregnancy.

Their expenses were far higher than ours and far higher than they expected. The laws in Tabasco, Mexico are clear that the surrogate cannot demand money for carrying your child beyond normal expenses. We agreed on a monthly stipend that excluded medical costs. We gave Karla additional money to pay for the monthly doctor visits and minor medical needs. We also reimbursed her for additional medical expenses that she incurred during the pregnancy, including blood transfusions, iron shots, and cold medications. This helped us keep costs in check.

Our relationship with Karla made it easy to keep costs in check. For example, Karla and I worked together to find lodging for her and her family in Villahermosa. Together we chose a place that wasn't the cheapest, but was far from the most expensive. It accommodated their needs for a fraction of what we would have paid for a hotel. Karla was able to call and get the in-country rates, which were about half what Americans are typically charged for the same type of accommodation.

Tips for Ensuring Yours is an Altruistic Surrogacy

Many agencies are still new to surrogacy in Mexico and may lead you down the wrong path, which could delay your return home with the child. We received the following guidelines from a smart Mexican Lawyer

1. Paying amounts beyond expenses can be construed as child trafficking.
2. Specify that you will cover expenses for the term you negotiate with the surrogate. (In our case, we agreed to pay expenses from the time Karla started preparation for IVF until one month after delivery.)
3. Set a limit for expenses based on the average food, shelter, and clothing costs you gathered during your investigation.
4. While you can use a third party to make the payments to the surrogate, it's better to pay the surrogate directly so she can cover expenses as they are incurred. We paid Karla through PayPal. Other surrogates have told us they prefer this approach because there have been cases in which agencies charged IPs for items such as lodging, food, and clothing, but the surrogate never received the money or received it much later than needed.
5. Keep receipts to prove that the expenses are legitimate. If you pay the surrogate expenses through an agency, clearly specify that the funds are for the surrogate's expenses and request proof she received them. Both the U.S. and Mexican governments may ask for receipts to prove that the arrangement is altruistic.

What to Expect with Surrogacy

This chapter provides a high-level view of the surrogacy and exit processes in Mexico and describes the players involved in each phase. Subsequent chapters go into more detail for each phase.

The Players *apply to Mexico*

There are a number of players whom you are likely to encounter on your journey through surrogacy process. Let's take a look at the role each one plays.

1. *U.S. immigration attorney.* Unless you have legal skills and knowledge of U.S. immigration laws, take the time to consult an attorney who can explain what you have to do to comply with applicable laws. Doing so will help you avoid roadblocks when it's time to bring your baby home.

2. *Mexican (or country of surrogacy) surrogacy attorney.* Surrogacy laws in Mexico differ substantially from U.S. laws. We highly recommend you also engage a lawyer who understands the country's surrogacy and child trafficking laws. The attorney should also be somewhat familiar with the general process for exit based on experience with other clients.

3. *IVF clinic.* For a surrogacy contract to be legal in Mexico, IPs must use a government-certified IVF clinic. The certification is called COFEPRIS, and a certified clinic will be able to provide you with its COFEPRIS permit number.

4. *OB/GYN and delivery doctor.* You'll need a reputable OB/GYN to monitor the pregnancy and deliver the baby. If the surrogate lives in Villahermosa, the same doctor can handle routine medical treatment during the pregnancy and delivery. If she lives somewhere else, you'll need an OB/GYN in her home town for the first seven months, and another one to handle the delivery in Villahermosa. Experience with surrogacy and multiple births is a plus for the OB/GYN(s).

5. *Pediatrician in Mexico.* Delivery doctors are associated with a hospital or clinic, and can recommend a pediatrician to care for your baby after birth, administer immunizations, and provide a health verification letter.

6. *Hospital in Mexico.* Delivery doctors are on staff at one or more hospitals and will give you the names. Check out the hospitals to see which one, in your opinion, has the best facilities and best care. It should be equipped

with a neonatal intensive care unit and facilities to care for the surrogate, infants, and IPs.

7. *Translator.* Unless you are fluent in Spanish, employ the services of a translator to help you understand all legal documents before you sign them; provide medical updates throughout the IVF process, pregnancy, and delivery; facilitate Skype and phone conversations with the surrogate; negotiate fees and costs with physicians, clinics, and others; and help you interact with government agencies to obtain a birth certificate, Mexican passport, and other activities required to take your baby home.

8. *Surrogate.* This is the woman who will carry your child to full term.

9. *U.S. consulate or embassy.* Embassy/consulate personnel process the immigration and citizenship papers that permit you to return to the U.S. with your child.

10. *Registro Civil (Civil Registry Office).* This Mexican government agency records and grants birth certificates.

11. *Secretary General.* Unless your contract is registered with this legal division of the Registro Civil, it is not legal and the Registro Civil cannot issue a birth certificate.

12. *Secretaría de Relaciones Exteriores (SRE)* — This Mexican equivalent of the U.S. State Department processes passports.

13. *Third-party agency (optional).* This third party subcontracts services on your behalf to the IVF clinic, in-country lawyer, delivery doctors, translators, and so forth. Some agencies match the IPs with a surrogate. We recommend that IPs participate as much as possible in finding and selecting the surrogate and understanding her circumstances.

14. *Egg and/or sperm donor (optional).* Egg donors donate eggs, anonymously or otherwise, for IPs who cannot supply their own eggs. Likewise, a sperm donor provides his sperm.

15. *Geneticist (optional).* The U.S. requires proof of a genetic link between at least one of the IPs and the child. While DNA testing isn't legally mandated, U.S. officials may insist that you do DNA testing using an AABB accredited lab in the U.S. The geneticist conducts the test for the lab.

The Process

Now that we've identified the key players, it's time to focus on the overall process, as illustrated in Figure 2.

Figure 2. The Surrogacy Process

Phase 1 - Investigation

During the investigation phase you determine your budget, family requirements, and the best path to move forward. During this phase, read everything you can find related to surrogacy in general and surrogacy in Mexico or the country you are interested in particular. Check out articles, blogs, and surrogacy websites. There are also surrogacy conferences. Take advantage of every resource to educate yourself on all the aspects of surrogacy abroad, including:

- Laws related to surrogacy in that country such as Mexico
- U.S. immigration requirements and processes
- Infant mortality rates

- Quality of healthcare/Reputation of potential clinics
- Treatment of surrogates
- Protections for IPs

Phase 2 - Selection

Your next step is to select not only a surrogate but also the service providers who will help you through the surrogacy process. Examples include:

- U.S. and Mexican attorneys
- Translator
- In-country agency or facilitator
- IVF doctor/clinic, OB/GYN, and pediatrician
- Delivery hospital

Some of these providers are essential, such as the IVF doctor, OB/GYN, pediatrician, and hospital. Others are optional, such as an agency or a translator.

Phase 3 - Contracts and Implantation

Before you move forward with implantation, execute all appropriate contracts and confirm that all parties can uphold their part of the agreement in fulfilling these contracts. The surrogate and IPs have to undergo a series of physical and psychological tests to prove suitability to perform their contractual obligations.

Phase 4 - Pregnancy and Planning for Delivery

Pregnancy and delivery planning activities involve supporting your surrogate financially and emotionally, ensuring she receives appropriate medical care, creating delivery plans and contingency plans, preparing your home for the baby, and putting plans in place for the delivery.

Phase 5 - Delivery and Birth Certificates

This phase covers the time period just before, during, and shortly after delivery. For children born in the U.S., birth certificates are typically issued at the hospital. For children born in Mexico, IPs must obtain birth certificates from the Registro Civil. The birth certificate process may vary per country.

Phase 6 – Exit (U.S. Citizenship and Mexican Passports)

In the exit phase, you obtain U.S. citizenship[12] and passports for your child. Although you can process your U.S. citizenship paperwork at the U.S. consulate or embassy offices in Merida (Tabasco), Tijuana (Baja), or Mexico City, we recommend Mexico City.

The SRE recommends that all children born in Mexico enter and exit the country with a Mexican passport. However, the current process to obtain the passport is onerous. At the time of this book's publication, processing time is two to four months. Ask advice of your Mexican or in-country attorney if this phase is required and what the appropriate steps are.

---

[12] The process used in Mexico is fundamentally the same as the process in India, and Thailand, except for restrictions on traditional surrogacy in Mexico.

Phase 1 – Investigation

As with any major life decision, the decision to have a child with the help of a surrogate should not be taken lightly. If you were buying a new car or planning a trip to Hawaii, you'd definitely do your homework. Researching the surrogacy journey is even more important. Keep in mind: An ounce of planning truly is worth ten pounds of cure. The Investigation phase is the most critical step in ensuring a smooth and successful surrogacy journey.

This section highlights key activities involved in investigating the appropriate route for surrogacy. We recommend you purchase a journal in which to record your activities as you move through the process.

Getting Started

Key areas to investigate as part of this first phase include:

- Personal choices and considerations
- Traditional surrogacy versus gestational substitute
- Considerations when going abroad
- Altruistic versus commercial surrogacy
- Laws regarding surrogacy and immigrating the child to the IPs' home country
- Citizenship and exit requirements for your country
- Using a middleman versus engaging an agency in the birth country
- What to look for in a surrogate

Figure 3 summarizes the questions you should answer to help you develop your requirements for surrogacy.

Figure 3. Questions to Answer in the Investigation Phase

If we need donor eggs or sperm, what are the desired traits? What traits are we unwilling to accept?

Are there translator services that can help us with our investigation?

What is the minimum quality we are willing to accept for the clinic, the hospital, and/or the surrogate's environment?

Are we ready to parent multiples?

What if the surrogate miscarries?

What does our budget look like, including IVF, surrogacy support, medical, agency, legal, citizenship, and exit processing fees?

Do we understand the laws of both countries and the implications of those laws?

Do we need a translator to interact with the surrogate, attorneys, doctors, and others?

Is there anything special we need to do to get citizenship?

Do we have time and ability to do the work ourselves or should we contract with an agency?

Do we need the help of a qualified attorney in Mexico? In the U.S.?

Do we require any special services or processes such as pregenetic determination to identify genetic defects, or sperm washing to increase the likelihood of one gender over another?

Personal Journey

As you start this very personal journey, there are questions that only you and your partner can answer. Your answers will shape the journey, so this is the most critical step you'll take. Set aside some uninterrupted time to discuss the questions in the nearby figures. It's likely you'll need to do this over a period of time as you and your partner explore your feelings and concerns about each question.

Figure 4. Questions for your Personal Journey — General

What are your personal beliefs on surrogacy?

What are your religious beliefs?

Is your relationship ready for the emotional toll of surrogacy and a new child?

Are you ready to parent multiples? If so how many embryos are you willing to transfer knowing each one could be viable?

Do you believe in abortion? Under what circumstances?

What will you do if the baby has a genetic disorder such as Down syndrome?[13]

If the surrogate miscarries, what do you want to do? How many tries can you afford emotionally and financially?

Is there a family member or friend who would be your surrogate?

What type of relationship do you want to have with the surrogate?

How will you communicate with the surrogate if you do not speak her language?

How do you plan to protect the surrogate's family if she dies in childbirth?

What languages do you speak? Do you have trustworthy friends or family members who speak the language of the surrogacy/birth country?

What countries do you feel comfortable exploring? Have you traveled there before? Do you have any concerns over safety?

What type of surrogacy is best for you based on your family needs and the laws of the birth country?

Figure 5. Questions for your Personal Journey — Donors

Do you need donor eggs or sperm? Do you need additional testing to find out?

How much money are you willing to spend on donors?

---

[13] According to Mexican law, the IPs are named as the parents of any child born as a result of a surrogacy contract. IPs can't change their minds after the child is born.

29

If you need donor eggs/sperm, what key characteristics/traits are you looking for in a donor?

- Hair color
- Eye color
- Skin color/tone
- Ethnicities
- Mouth or facial features
- Body type/build (include body mass index)
- Family genetic/medical history – what are you willing to accept or not accept. For example, you may specify you are not willing to accept a donor with a history of mental illness or genetic disorders.
- IQ
- Career

Figure 6. Questions for your Personal Journey — Care Considerations

How much are you willing to assist the surrogate during the pregnancy? During recovery?

In case of an emergency, is there someone who can take time off to care for the baby and surrogate? (This can be an IP or family member.)

How much can you afford to spend?

What expenses does your health insurance cover?

Are any expenses tax deductible?

It's okay to start additional investigation activities before you've answered every question. The key is to work through the questions so when the clinics, doctors, and agencies start asking you for specifics, you'll be prepared.

Considerations for IPs from Other Countries

This book provides insights based on our experience with the U.S. and Mexico. Although we don't have direct experience with surrogacy outside of the U.S./Mexico combination other than initial investigation and surrogate interview, we have helped IPs from other countries, including Canada, Germany,

The Netherlands, and France, by sharing what we know about the surrogacy process.

It's important to understand what you are getting into and how it impacts you. Don't leave it to a facilitator or agency to provide accurate information on your country and the country where the surrogacy will take place. Do your own research.

If Surrogacy is not Legal in your Country

If your country's laws prohibit surrogacy, don't pursue it without making sure you have a clear path for taking your baby home. Confirm everything with attorneys familiar with the laws of your country and the birth country.

Germany, The Netherlands, France, and other countries have surrogacy laws that are stricter than those of the U.S. Each country has provided a path for IPs to bring the child home as long as there is a genetic link to the father. In some cases, the country of origin has required that the intended mother complete a step-parent adoption in their courts.

The Mexican government delays passport approvals of passports because officials want to ensure that the laws of Mexico and of the IPs' home country are being followed. Their heightened reviews and concerns stem from cases such as a Spanish couple that did not comply with laws of Spain. The Spanish government refused to grant citizenship to the baby and the couple was left stranded in Mexico. There are other cases of Canadian and U.S. couples that did not comply with Mexican laws and then blamed Mexico for delays in processing their paperwork. For more information on these cases, visit https://www.facebook.com/pages/Surrogacy-In-Mexico-debunking-facts-from-fiction/385820588227450?sk=events.

Don't be the First

The first agency we worked with led us to believe that Mexico was a mature market for foreign IPs. While IVF and surrogacy are mature markets for Mexican citizens and some medical facilities have expertise in dealing with surrogacy, the processes for the U.S. government (and others) to grant citizenship were not at the time we started our journey. The surrogacy process is well documented and understood in countries such India. However, that doesn't mean countries such as Nepal or Cambodia will handle surrogacy for foreign IPs in the same way. If you go first, you'll be paving the way. You'll have to bear the burden of paying and experiencing delays while the people involved learn what to do. We found this to be expensive not only in terms of money but time away from our home. If you deal with service providers, be sure to get three references of IPs from your country who have successfully completed the exit process.

What to Look For in an Agency and/or Facilitator

This section is based on the lessons we learned as a result of working directly with multiple agencies and facilitators, including excellent ones such as Imer, Insemer, and La Cigüeña del Bebé.

Let's start with the difference between a facilitator and an agency providing surrogacy services. Sometimes it's difficult to tell the difference because facilitators often advertise themselves as agencies. However, facilitators do not provide services directly. They are individuals or organizations that resell the services of service providers in the birth country. That is, they resell the services of surrogacy agencies, IVF clinics, delivery doctors, translators, and others.

Some facilitators and agencies are reputable and highly knowledgeable, and they do a good job of guiding IPs through the surrogacy process. Others are in learning mode. They are sincere in their efforts and will make every attempt to do a good job. There are some facilitators and agencies, however, who are simply trying to make a fast buck.

A July 27, 2014 *New York Times* article on Planet Hospital, "An Agency that Delivers Heartache,"[14] confirmed that IPs need to watch out for facilitators and agencies trying to line their pockets at the IPs' expense. Planet Hospital is currently under investigation by the U.S. Federal Bureau of Investigation for fraud. Mr. Rupak, a Planet Hospital founder, said, "There is a lot of treachery and deception in I.V.F./fertility/surrogacy because there is gobs of money to be made."

---

[14] "An Agency that Delivers Heartache," http://www.nytimes.com/2014/07/28/us/surrogacy-agency-planet-hospital-delivered-heartache.html?_r=0

A good facilitator or agency isn't only in the business of selling surrogacy. Surrogacy is a small part of the larger business of infertility. There are other routes that couples can take. A facilitator or agency that understands each route can act as a trusted advisor, offering you multiple options instead of trying to sell you on surrogacy.

So how do you decide which agencies are good and which are not? After interviews and discussions with several agencies, we've come up with three categories:

1. Experienced with surrogacy in Mexico (or the country of surrogacy)
2. Inexperienced with surrogacy in that country but honest and trying to learn
3. Cavalier – inexperienced and willing to say/do anything to get into the business without considering the impact on the IPs or surrogate

Imer, Insemer, and La Cigüeña del Bebé are examples of category 1. Staff members were upfront about what they knew and what they didn't know. They were willing to work with us the entire way to learn the intricacies of surrogacy in Mexico. They were highly familiar with Mexican surrogacy laws, which was critical to our overall success. They had other clients willing to provide testimonials and references to speak for their work and dedication. We never felt ignored, alone, or concerned after we signed on with them.

Another agency that assisted us, International Child Foundation, falls into category 2. They knew a lot about adoption and the laws of Mexico regarding adoption. They made it clear they didn't have in-depth knowledge about surrogacy. They offered to assist us at no charge for the areas in which they were knowledgeable. In return, we allowed them to follow our case. They reached out to the Mexican agencies we were working with and tried to learn as much as possible about surrogacy in Mexico.

Our first agency (in the U.S.) falls into category 3. They communicate misinformation because they haven't taken the time to understand the market, the process, or the requirements for success. Category 3 individuals and companies all had similar characteristics:

1. *Self serving.* They ruthlessly promote themselves in social media sites, at the expense of others if necessary. Yet they have no actual experience they can point to. They typically can't provide references.
2. *Lack of accountability.* They change the game or business model along the way without being accountable. Our first agency claimed we were never clients. However, we have proof that we had engaged the agency's services.
3. *Business model that lacks concern for surrogates and IPs.* These entities encourage IPs to set up escrow accounts and pay all fees up front. IPs should have the option to pay the surrogate, doctors, and others either directly *or* through the agency.
4. *Primary motive is money.* An agency that quotes a price of more than $50,000 (not including travel) is probably charging more than it should. Our costs, including travel, medical, surrogate-related expenses, and extra for twins and medical complications, were only $34,000. Note this excludes extra travel and time in country not related to the surrogacy.

What to Look for in a Surrogate

Picking your surrogate is one of the most critical steps in your journey. It is important that, as a couple, you discuss the characteristics that are important to you and determine where it's critical for you and your spouse to be on the same page, and where you are willing to compromise. With the excitement of finally being able to have a baby, you may overlook critical details that could lead to issues later.

Surrogates in Mexico are similar in some ways to those in the U.S. and other countries. However, there are differences. Some may be desperate and motivated by money. Others like Karla are looking to help a couple wanting to expand their family. The internet gives all of them access to forums in locations where commercial surrogacy is legal and easily accessible. Surrogates may not understand the laws in their own country and may mislead IPs into arrangements that are problematic. Any arrangement that appears commercial in nature is illegal in Mexico.

Mexican laws are designed to prevent child trafficking. Surrogates and egg donors have certain privacy rights that cannot be violated. You can ask about physical characteristics such as height, eye color, and hair color. During the selection process, however, you cannot look at photos of the surrogate or egg donor. An agency that gives you a catalog picturing donors or surrogates is breaking the law. If you are finding your own surrogate through Facebook, surrogacy communities, or other online sources in Mexico, they typically cannot show you pictures of the surrogates. Nothing prevents the surrogate from posting her own picture on foreign sites. The key is that IPs cannot discriminate or select a surrogate or egg donor based on looks alone.

Once you have been matched with a potential surrogate or egg donor you can ask for a picture and a face-to-face meeting. After meeting the surrogate, if you believe the surrogate is not a match for your family, you can consider other surrogates.

Characteristics of a Good Surrogate

A good surrogate is financially stable. That means she can support herself and her family based on current income. She shouldn't be completely dependent on the money she receives from the surrogacy to live. If she can afford to support herself, then the surrogacy provides living expenses for a period of time, enabling her to put aside some of her own money, which she can use to improve her quality of life after the surrogacy. Once the baby is born and the relationship winds down, the surrogate needs to be able to return to the life she had before the pregnancy.

A clean medical history is also essential. Mexican law requires that surrogacy candidates submit to a lab test for STDs. Also, Mexico has a high rate of anemia during pregnancy. According to one study, the rate could be as high as 20 percent.[15] Consequently, it's important to check iron levels. You don't necessarily rule out a surrogate due to low iron levels. However, the information helps you determine who is a better candidate and alerts you to the fact that additional medications or treatments may be required.

Good surrogates have already had at least one child and don't plan to have more children of their own. This is important because complications as a result

---

[15] http://www.redalyc.org/articulo.oa?id=10612586006

35

of the pregnancy could result in the surrogate not being able to have additional children.

Previous pregnancies can also identify the potential for complications such as gestational diabetes or anemia. Previous C-sections should also be of concern, because multiples are common with surrogacy, which increases the likelihood that a C-section will be necessary.

Look for someone who is emotionally, mentally, and physically stable. The surrogate needs to be at peace with the fact the child she will bear belongs to someone else. A woman who has never had children may have difficulty giving up the child after the birth. This decision to give up the child could complicate things. Mental health issues such as depression and schizophrenia could also lead to complications for the baby and your journey overall.

Another factor to consider is the surrogate's body mass index (BMI). A BMI below 31 is advisable because women with higher BMIs are more prone to blood clotting, cancer, and other medical issues caused by the medications needed to undergo IVF and to support the pregnancy for the first 12 weeks.

Budgeting and Expenses

You'll need to consider many items in your budget, including but not limited to legal services, travel, medication, medical (IVF, checkups, delivery, emergencies, hospital stay, and vaccinations), surrogate living expenses, your travel and living expenses in Mexico, Skype and/or phone service, passports, visas, and citizenship and immigration processing fees. The amounts included in this section are rough estimates based on our personal experience and research from social media sites.[16] It's important to track expenses against your budget and be aware if costs are higher than budgeted. Otherwise costs can spiral out of control.

One word of caution: Many Mexican surrogates who sign up on social media sites want to receive payment like surrogates in the U.S. This is unrealistic due to Mexico's significantly lower cost of living and legal mandates for altruistic surrogacy.

---

[16] Take into account inflation and currency rate fluctuations.

Agencies often try to combine all expense items into one big package that can result in much higher costs. We've seen quotes and advertised prices that vary from $40,000 to $80,000 just for the surrogacy. Travel, citizenship processing, passports, and other costs are extra. These quotes seem outrageous to us considering that our total costs were around $34,000, excluding the additional costs we incurred due to U.S. immigration issues.

Don't get caught off-guard by agencies trying to charge rates equivalent to those in the U.S. One couple we spoke to were quoted $13,000 by an agency for donor eggs, whereas input we received from IPs who got quotes directly from Mexican clinics indicates that donor eggs don't cost more than $800 per harvest. Multiple IPs have told us about agencies that marked up other services such as psychological screening, travel, hotel accommodations for the surrogate, travel for donors from other countries, maternity clothes, and transportation from the airport.

Moreover, some of the agencies never delivered services that were included in the contract and that IPs paid for. The IPs weren't able to recover their money because the cost for taking legal action was too high or the agency became insolvent (as did Planet Hospital). There have also been cases of agencies putting the IPs' and surrogate's expense money in an escrow account, embezzling the funds, and leaving the IPs and pregnant surrogates to get through the remainder of the process on their own.

We strongly believe that going *à la carte* and using a trustworthy translator who is familiar with the process and the country is far better for IPs and the surrogate. Here's the route we recommend based on what we did after firing our first agency and reading about Planet Hospital:

1. Hire a translator who is familiar with medical tourism.
2. Hire a reputable Mexican attorney.
3. Contract with each party directly using a Mexican attorney.
4. Keep copies of all contracts to help you track when services and payments are due.
5. Pay each party through PayPal or by wire transfer.

37

6. Minimize your exposure by never paying 100 percent up front and avoid paying cash.

Surrogate Expenses ($8,000-$15,000)

Although the surrogate provides the most in terms of time and attention for your developing baby, never forget that it's an altruistic arrangement. Understanding what the surrogate's expenses are is critical. The low end of the $8,000 to $15,000 range covers expenses for a single mother of one. The high end includes extras for an extended family. Expenses include food, utilities, transportation to and from the clinic, travel to Villahermosa, lodging in the surrogate's hometown and in Villahermosa where the baby will be born, clothing, and many miscellaneous items. Note we had gotten visas for our surrogate, her fiancé, daughter and extended family to come to the US to have the baby. Those are part of our expenses but our surrogate's visa was not approved prior to delivery.

An emergency fund is important to cover unexpected expenses. Giving the surrogate $200 cash to keep on hand for emergencies is beneficial for all parties. Our emergency fund came in handy several times for additional iron shots and other unanticipated medical expenses. Remember, surrogates can get sick and, because they are pregnant, they may require an elevated level of care to ensure your baby is well cared for. This approach also gave the surrogate the flexibility of having funds on hand for medical emergencies, which resulted in a more tranquil pregnancy.

We investigated monthly living expenses in our surrogate's hometown and used that information to come up with a monthly stipend. We listed expenses and discussed amounts with the surrogate and explained what we would and would not cover. As a result, there were no surprises.

In our case, the stipend was approximately $800 to $1,100 to support Karla, Ian, and their daughter. We provided a higher amount when she was in Villahermosa so she could keep her condo in Tijuana to return back to after the babies were born. As discussed earlier, we did some work on their condo, which meant she and her family had a nicer and safer place to live.

We increased the stipend for the time in Villahermosa to include the additional cost of lodging there, taxi service to and from the clinic, and eating out more often. We kept expenses down by using PayPal to give Karla the funds to book and pay for rooms. She was able to get local rates because she spoke fluent Spanish and was native to Mexico.

In Villahermosa, we spent a little under $600 per month for lodging for Karla, a savings of over $500 per month compared to what we found on U.S. sites. Other costs in Villahermosa were about $600 a month more because we covered the cost of her fiancé to travel with her to care for her while she was in Villahermosa. Note we used the recommended travel expense per diem published by companies for daily meals when travelling in that area of Mexico.

Another critical item We recommend purchasing is life insurance for the surrogate. That insurance provides for the financial security of her family in the event the pregnancy or delivery causes the death of the surrogate. (Although life insurance is legal, health insurance for the surrogate is not legal in Mexico.)

Medical Expenses ($12,000-$30,000)

Medical expenses vary significantly based on agency fees, how well you negotiate, how well you know what things cost in Mexico (for example, donor eggs), and how savvy you are with respect to currency exchange rates. We shopped around and received quotes from three facilities for IVF and delivery. We chose an IVF clinic in Tijuana because it was convenient for us to get to and significantly cut down the travel costs for us to make several trips there during the pregnancy.

This section does not include costs associated with medical complications. It's a good idea to set aside an additional $10,000 for unexpected medical expenses.

IVF

IVF costs range from $8,000 to $15,000, based on our experience and inputs from other IPs. Although this number appears to be high, at the time we underwent IVF, implantation attempts in the U.S. cost approximately $25,000 each. Some IPs told us they were charged an additional $2,000 above and beyond the IVF cost in Mexico to freeze embryos. Not all agencies provide embryo freezing, so we recommend you ask how much it costs if they do offer this service. Several IPs told us there was a charge for embryo freezing on their delivery bill. In at least one case, the IPs were not aware that this service had been provided.

Additional costs related to IVF include medicines and psychological evaluations needed for matching IPs with a gestational substitute. Prescreening tests at the lab for our surrogate, Paul, and me were about $600.

Doctor Visits

Monthly doctor visits run about $40 to $50 each for a total of about $400. These are routine visits. Plan for additional expenditures for various medical conditions that might develop, including urinary tract infections, anemia, ruptured belly button, back pain, nerve issues, and even the common cold. We paid $600 to $1,250 per blood transfusion when Karla developed anemia and needed four transfusions.

Delivery

Delivery costs vary from one hospital to another. The range was $3,000 to $4,000 for a normal delivery with 50 percent more for a second child. If you're expecting triplets or more, check on additional costs at the hospital, which may include bassinet rentals, pediatrician services, and so forth. Several IPs told us that the agencies they have interviewed mark up the delivery of twins by as much as 100 percent.

Legal Expenses ($2,500 to $6,000)

Attorney fees were all over the map in Mexico. We interviewed six different lawyers. We chose Cristina Valdez who is associated with La Cigüeña del Bebé because the others had very limited experience with Mexico's surrogacy laws. While there are many advice forums and other places for finding an independent attorney, this is an area of the law in which it is hard to find someone with experience.

A knowledgeable lawyer makes a huge difference in getting you through the process and ensuring you can take your child home. It's worth paying extra for someone with experience not only in surrogacy but also child trafficking laws. Experienced surrogacy attorneys understand the costs involved and charge accordingly instead of constantly hitting you with unanticipated additional charges as they encounter them.

We cannot stress enough the importance of a lawyer who understands not only State of Tabasco laws but also Mexican federal laws regulating IVF and child trafficking. We've counseled a number of IPs who found themselves stuck in Mexico because their lawyer failed to follow the law.

A U.S. immigration attorney who specializes in surrogacy can help with the immigration process. It isn't necessary to put this lawyer on retainer. However, meeting the attorney and getting a consultation is a wise move because then you'll have someone available if you need legal assistance.

Translator ($2,500-$6,000)

Although some doctors and lawyers speak English, very few nurses, hospital staff, and Mexican officials do. Although I am fluent in Spanish, I struggled at times with the medical and legal terminology as well as with regional idioms and pronunciation. We were fortunate that Ian is an English teacher and was able to assist us in this area.

Agencies, clinics, hospitals, and other service providers often have translation services. However, it's well worth the money to hire an independent translator to review and translate contracts and assist with such activities as getting Mexican passports and birth certificates.

Translators can provide concierge services for everything from booking rooms to scheduling appointments. Examples include:

- Assisting with interviews of IVF clinics, doctors, and lawyers
- Reviewing all contracts
- Identifying cheaper rates for hotels, airlines, and places to stay
- Interpreting for interviews with the Registro Civil and SRE

Translators also ensure you understand exactly what you are signing by explaining all contract terms in English. Although reputable agencies and lawyers don't try to trick you into signing something you shouldn't, it's good to have someone in your corner to keep them from making mistakes.

41

It's also smart to have a translator who lives close to the surrogate and can check on her periodically and make sure her living conditions haven't changed or that other aspects of her life might put her or the baby at risk.

You will likely pay extra, including airfare and lodging, if you want your translator to help with government processes such as obtaining Mexican passports. An in-country attorney may provide a service to help in this area.

Agency Fees (A Percentage of Medical/Legal Fees, up to $35,000)

Agency fee structures and charges vary substantially. Agency fee structures range from a "free" service, in which the agency receives a percentage of the doctor and lawyer fees, to a schedule of fees for administrative services, matching, social services, donor eggs, psychological testing, clothing, and other services. The important thing is to decide if the services the agency provides address your needs and if there are any hidden costs such as markups for surrogate travel or donor eggs that inflate the price of an all-inclusive package. If you're paying a middleman, your costs will be higher.

Travel Expenses ($5,000-$20,000)

Most agencies don't tell the full story about the travel expenses required for a successful surrogacy abroad. Travel is the biggest variable. It breaks down into phases: investigation, IVF, and delivery. Although not all IPs travel to Mexico or the country of surrogacy during the investigation phase, it's a good idea to meet the various agencies, doctors, attorneys, and your surrogate in person, and to visit the clinics and hospitals.

Travel expenses vary considerably depending on your location and the locations of the people you meet with. It cost us approximately $800 per trip to drive from Arizona to Tijuana. Because we were relatively close to the IVF clinic it was convenient and not too costly. If things go wrong and you have to spend more time in Mexico, or make multiple trips, travel expenses will naturally be higher.

Include costs to fly from your home city to Villahermosa for the contract execution and the birth, and to Mexico City for the U.S. citizenship and immigration process. Plan for emergencies: You may have to make extra trips, and you may have to change your air travel plans. Our change fees to fly to Villahermosa for our daughters' early birth were approximately $400.

The cost to fly Karla, Ian, and their daughter to Villahermosa for the birth and then back to Tijuana was approximately $1,000. This included change fees because they had to travel earlier due to anemia issues. Later we learned that it's less expensive to book the flights within Mexico. That reduces international travel rates and change fees.

Another way we saved money was using our airline miles for a hotel room and rental car. There are many nice hotels in Villahermosa. Paul and I stayed at a local place Karla found online that was only $500 per month.

Finally, although taxis are an option for transportation around Villahermosa and Mexico City, you should consider renting a car. (Taxis are more readily available in Mexico City.) Once the baby is born, you'll find a rental car is more convenient and, when the weather is warm, the air conditioning will be a blessing.

Payment of Expenses

IPs can pay for expenses in a variety of ways, including cash for small expenditures such as meals, taxis, or photocopies. We suggest wire transfers or PayPal for larger expenses. Be sure to consider fees associated with paying expenses, including exchange rates for cash and transaction fees for wire transfers and PayPal. We advise against overusing your credit card or ATM card in Mexico because you are charged a foreign transaction fee each time you swipe the card. Those fees can add up and your bank probably won't offer you the best exchange rate.

Phase 2 - Selection Phase

Now that you have done your homework, the selection phase should go smoothly. We recommend that you create a comparison matrix for the providers that you're considering. Include characteristics you have defined as critical as well as those that are nice to have. Rank each provider on a scale of one to five for each characteristic.[17]

During the selection phase, follow the Rule of 3: Get at least three quotes and three references from each provider. Contact the references and discuss their experiences with the provider. By talking to the references you can develop a sense of which provider is the best fit for your situation.

Egg Donor

If you require an egg donor, pay close attention to Mexican child trafficking laws, which require anonymity for egg donors to prevent the creation of designer babies. You can look at a picture of a potential donor's mouth, eyes, or other body parts, but not of the entire face or body. Couples we worked with who used egg donors told us that once they selected the donor they were able to speak with her on the phone to find out more about family medical history and donor characteristics and interests.

Egg donors can be Mexican citizens or women who travel to Mexico from other countries. The price varies from $800 to $4,000 for a Mexican donor to $18,000 for one from the U.S. The markup on donated eggs can be substantial and misrepresentations can occur. It's hard to tell at first blush if you are being overcharged.

Insist on interviewing the egg donor to ensure she is from the location indicated by the agency. Although you can't see pictures of the egg donor, once you select her, you can ask to learn more about her background.

Another option is to find your own egg donor online if you want one from your country or of a specific race or nationality. This approach cuts out the middleman, eliminating markup on services.

---

[17] For sample matrices, visit our blog at https://www.facebook.com/pages/Surrogacy-In-Mexico-debunking-facts-from-fiction/385820588227450

Key areas to ask the donor about include ethnicity and country of origin; hair color, eye color, height, weight, and body mass index; occupation; and education. Also obtain a full medical history from the donor and her family. The best approach is to ask your doctor (or your pediatrician in your home country) for a medical history form. Have the donor answer all questions. On your child's first visit to his or her pediatrician in the U.S., give the doctor a copy of the form for your child's file.

The Surrogate

While I was in college, I studied the work of Victoria Molfese, a renowned perinatal/prenatal psychologist. Dr. Molfese's studies tracked child development during the formative years. Many people do not realize that a human being's personality starts to develop as early as five months in the womb and is nearly 80 percent complete by age five. Many studies show that during gestation the sounds, attitude of the mother, and environment have an impact on the development of a child.

Because of Molfese's findings, we believe that choosing the surrogate and the environment the baby will be exposed to for the nine months in the womb is critical. So it's important to find the right surrogate for your family. We identified 13 prospective surrogates and spent a lot of time on this step. We put together questions about general medical history, family information, and so forth, and sent them to these women to come up with a shortlist of good candidates.

Eliminate Candidates with Red Flags

Prospective surrogates' answers to some questions may raise red flags that help you narrow down your list. For example, one surrogate we considered insisted on using her own eggs. Given she lived in a state in the U.S. where surrogacy contracts are not recognized, we decided she wasn't a good fit. In general, eliminate anyone who appears too interested in financial gain or insists on using her own genetic material. Also eliminate anyone who doesn't share your beliefs about abortion and genetic defects.

45

After you identify the top candidates, plot their proximity to your location. Closer proximity is important because of travel costs and the possibility you will need to travel to the surrogate's location on short notice.

Narrow your list to three women and interview them. We went through this process several times because some candidates answered the questionnaire very well, but did not interview well. If we felt the chemistry wasn't right, we would move on to the next candidate on our list.

We interviewed 13 candidates but always ended up coming back to Karla, who was one of the first three we interviewed. On average, IPs interview three to four women before they find the right surrogate.

Some agencies try to select the surrogate for you. It's fine for the agency to help, but it's up to you to ensure she's right for you. We looked at surrogates both in the U.S. and in Mexico. One option to reduce costs but still have the surrogacy in the U.S. is to select an American surrogate, take her to Mexico for IVF, and have her deliver in the U.S. It may be more expensive than going through the entire surrogacy process in Mexico. However, depending on your proximity to Mexico, it could bring down your overall costs in the US.

The Interview

Most people cannot maintain a false façade for more than 45 minutes in an interview. So, to get a feel for the real person, be sure the interview lasts at least an hour. Engage the surrogate in a comfortable conversation about her family, your family, and what each hopes to gain from the surrogacy relationship.

Consider the fact that the surrogate will always be part of your life. Whether you stay in contact with her or not, you will always think about her, especially when your child grows old enough to ask about his or her story. The child may wonder what happened to this woman. So, during the interview, determine if this is a person you want to be part of your life and your child's life.

If you are interviewing surrogates from a clinic, interview at least three and use an independent translator if they do not speak your language. You'll get more honest answers from an independent translator than from someone who works for the clinic and is probably trained on what to say. We conducted the initial interviews via Skype. Once we picked our top candidate we traveled to meet her in person. **Note we did not use an agency to find our surrogate as we wanted to insure the person we picked was someone we would be comfortable being a permanent part of our lives.

Figure 7 lists questions you can use for interviewing potential surrogates.

Figure 7. Sample Questions for Prospective Surrogates

How old are you?

What is your annual income? Expenses?

What is your current employment?

Do you have a partner? What is his current employment?

How frequently do you and your partner have relations? Is he willing to be tested for STDs?

Where do you live? Who lives with you? Please list all family members.

How does your family feel about you being a surrogate?

Who will assist you if you become ill or bedridden?

Can you provide photos of your home?

Do you own a car? If not, how will you get to the clinic and to medical checkups?

Do you have a checking account or PayPal account?

Does your medical history include any of the following?

- Cancer
- Anemia
- Heart conditions
- STDs
- Diabetes
- Allergies

Do you smoke, use drugs (including prescription drugs), or drink alcohol? If so, how often?

How often do you exercise?

What is your weight and height? (Use an online calculator to calculate BMI.)

How many children have you given birth to? Your own? Surrogate?

What are the ages of your children?

Who will care for your child(ren) when you are away for IVF procedures, medical treatments, and delivery?

How many C-sections have you had?

Do you have a history of anemia or gestational diabetes during pregnancy?

Have you ever traveled? Can you travel for IVF procedures and delivery?

Do you have a visa for the U.S. or any other country? If so, which countries?

What are your religious beliefs?

Do you believe in abortion?

What if the baby is deformed or has a major genetic defect?

Do you have a birth preference (vaginal or C-section)?

Are you willing to carry twins or triplets? Do you have any restrictions on the number of embryos to implant?

Do you have any uterine or other physical deformities that may prevent you from natural childbirth or carrying multiples?

What is your blood type? RH factor for your blood type?

Do you have a preference for either traditional surrogacy or gestational substitute?

Do you have internet access, cell phone, and/or a smart device for Skype sessions?

How often do you want to communicate with us during the pregnancy? After?

IVF/Delivery Location Choices

Now that you have selected your surrogate, it's time to consider your options in terms of the best route to a successful pregnancy and delivery. As Figure 8 illustrates, IVF can take place in Mexico and delivery can take place either in Villahermosa, Tabasco, or at location of your choosing in the U.S. Here are the options:

- IVF in Mexico with a surrogate who is a U.S. citizen; delivery in U.S.
- IVF in Mexico with Mexican surrogate; delivery in U.S. (if she has a visa)
- IVF in Mexico with Mexican surrogate, delivery in Mexico

Figure 8. Alternative Routes from IVF to Delivery

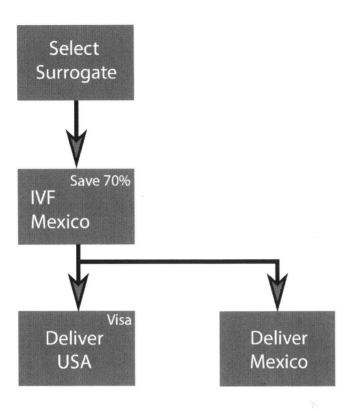

Originally, we planned to undergo IVF in Mexico and have Karla travel to the U.S. for delivery. One of the main reasons is that Mexican IVF clinics implant fresh instead of frozen embryos, so the success rate for pregnancy on the first attempt is higher. Another reason we wanted to take this route is that IVF is typically one of the bigger surrogacy expenses in the U.S. and health insurance doesn't always cover it.

We had to change course, however, because although we applied for Karla's visa before she was pregnant, the U.S. consulate did not issue the visa until after she gave birth. Our *à la carte* approach paid off in this situation because we had exception plans in place to protect us legally.

Delivery in the U.S.

If your surrogate already has a visa to enter the U.S. or is a U.S. citizen, your baby can be born either in the U.S. or Mexico. If she gives birth in the U.S., you don't have to apply for U.S. citizenship. The intended mother, however, does have to go through a step-parent adoption as part of the process. Step-parent adoptions typically are not as rigorous as traditional adoptions, and they don't cost as much.

The medical expenses in the U.S. are significantly higher than in Mexico. However, if your surrogate is a U.S. citizen, then it's possible to get health insurance for her. Insurance would bring down the cost of delivery and other procedures, thereby reducing your total expenses.

If your surrogate is Mexican and does not have a U.S. social security number, you may have a hard time getting health insurance for her in the US and health insurance is not legal for the surrogate in Mexico. The legal fees for adoption in the U.S. are about $5,000. The additional costs for travel and living expenses for the surrogate in Villahermosa may make up for the difference in medical deductibles and offset additional surrogacy costs.

Delivery in Mexico

Delivery in Villahermosa is the other option. Costs for this option may be higher than delivering with health insurance in the U.S., especially if multiple members of your family travel to Mexico for the birth. You should also travel to Villahermosa long before delivery to visit hospitals, so that you can choose the one that best fits your requirements. At the time of this book's publication, IPs are required to travel to Villahermosa to execute the surrogacy contract, so this visit is the best time to visit hospitals.

Translator

You can find translation services at universities and online.

Figure 9 is a list of questions to ask to help you choose a translator.

Figure 9. Questions to Ask Prospective Translators

How long have you been a translator? What languages do you speak?

What qualifications do you have?

How many clients do you have?

Do you have other employment? If so, what is it?

Have you translated for U.S. citizens in medical tourism before?

How familiar are you with surrogacy and the legal processes involved?

What do you charge?

How do you assist with the process?

What parts of Mexico are you willing to travel to? Is there a difference in cost for in-person versus online translations?

How do I reach you when I need your services?

Do you have Skype or other voice-over-IP communications to reduce long distance calling?

Agency/Facilitator

There are good facilitators and full-service agencies and clinics in the U.S. and Mexico. To find them, you have to do your homework and make sure that the agencies and individuals you select are more interested in you, your baby, and your surrogate than in lining their pockets. Many people who act as facilitators or work for agencies don't have medical training, they don't speak the language of all the countries they cover, and they don't understand surrogacy laws and processes.

A number of third-party facilitators call themselves agencies. However, instead of doing the work themselves, they subcontract everything to an agency in the country where the surrogacy takes place. If you deal with a third-party facilitator, you have to vet the facilitator and any providers they recommend.
51

Careful vetting can make the difference between bliss and bankruptcy for your family. During the process, we ran across agencies that endorsed themselves on other websites they owned, tried to trick us into providing information about our case by posing as U.S. embassy personnel, and tried to attach themselves to our case to promote a service they had never provided. Other IPs had even worse experiences. The *New York Times* article on Planet Hospital several examples of IPs who remained childless after spending exorbitant amounts of money.

Mexican lawyers, translators, and agency personnel cannot accompany you to the U.S. embassy to assist with the citizenship and immigration processes. That means they won't be able to advise you on what to do. If you're working with a U.S. agency, on the other hand, that agency isn't likely to have representatives in Mexico to help you when you go to the Registro Civil and the SRE.

The Investigation Phase chapter provides critical information on what makes a good agency/facilitator. Refer to that chapter as you work through your selection. Watch for red flags. Some of the "don'ts" below are covered in earlier chapters, but they are worth repeating:

- Don't view photos of surrogates or donors before you select one. Doing so violates Mexican privacy laws. Once you've made your selection, you can see photos if the surrogate or donor agrees to it.
- Don't offer (or pay for) health insurance for a surrogate in Mexico. (However, purchasing life insurance for a surrogate is legal.)
- Don't believe an agency that promises a 100 percent guarantee of pregnancy.
- Don't agree to egg splitting (using same egg donor for multiple IPs).
- Don't take the embryo adoption/donation route.
- Don't accept embryos created at clinic that doesn't have a COFEPRIS permit or that cannot affirm that embryo creation complied with Mexican child trafficking laws.
- Don't start the IVF process before executing and notarizing the gestational agreement in Tabasco, Mexico.
- Don't have anything in your surrogacy contract or take any action that can be construed as commercial surrogacy.
- Don't agree to sign a contract with a facilitator unless they are willing to indemnify you for any issues due to their errors or omissions.

The best way to avoid trouble is to ask the right questions. Figure 10 provides a list of questions to help you in your vetting process.

Figure 10. Questions to Ask Potential Facilitators and Agencies.

For how many years have you provided surrogacy services to U.S. citizens?
How many successful exits have you participated in?
Can you provide a list of at least three references that have successfully completed the exit process and three that are currently going through it?
Are you or is anyone on your staff fluent in Spanish or local language of country?
What benefits in terms of savings — cost, time, or effort — will your agency guarantee in the contract?
What remediation will you provide if you do not deliver on your commitments?
Can you provide documentation on the process and list the key contacts for each step?
Can you provide samples of psychological screening questionnaires for surrogates along with the credentials of the person who created them?
What are the living arrangements for the surrogate?
How do you find surrogates?
What is the screening process for STDs, psychological health, and environment readiness?
Do you subcontract services to anyone else? If so, to whom?
Can I pay the surrogate directly for her expenses?
Do you facilitate calls with the surrogate, doctors, and other key players? If so, how often?
When is the last time you were in Mexico?
Can you provide proof that you have visited the agency, clinics, hospitals, and doctors in person? (A copy of the *tramite* or airline records might help.)
What are the average expenses for travel during each phase? How do you facilitate travel?
Can you provide the credentials and information on the lawyer your agency/clinic uses?

What do you consider to be the top 10 mistakes that have led to issues in the exit process? In the pregnancy? In the birth certificate process? What services do you offer to avoid them?

Can you guarantee a successful exit and provide an indemnification clause in the contract if there are issues due to negligence on your part?

If you engage with an agency that provides all-inclusive services, you will also ask the questions in the next section on hospitals and physicians.

Hospitals and Physicians

The quality of medical care is a big concern for IPs seeking surrogacy services abroad. Figure 11 lists questions to help you in selecting the clinic, hospital, and delivery doctors.

Figure 11. Questions to Ask Hospitals and Physicians

IVF Doctors/Clinics

How do you require IPs to pay for services?

Who is your business manager?

Is medication included in the quoted costs?

Can you show me the COFEPRIS permit and/or your medical license?

What are the cleaning procedures for the fertilization instruments used by the embryologists?

What is the first-time success rate of the IVF clinic?

Are embryos frozen for additional tries? If so what are the costs and limitations?

In the case of fresh implantations, what happens to leftover embryos?

Where did your physicians receive their medical training? For how long? What additional specialties do they have?

Delivery Doctors/Hospital

How do you require IPs to pay for services?

Who is your business manager?

What is the cost for multiples? Do you negotiate?

What is the daily rate for the ICU? What percentage of infants end up in the ICU and what is the average cost?

What is the morbidity and mortality health grade of the hospital? Doctor? Can you provide an independent third party to verify the grade?

When can we tour the hospital and meet the doctors?

What sanitation and other precautions/training is provided to ensure a sterile environment in the operating/delivery room and neonatal care?

What translation services do you provide when hospital staff, physicians, business staff (billing), lawyers, and others don't speak English?

Will someone meet us at the airport to take us to the hospital?

What hospital services are included in the fee?

What should we bring with us for the baby (food, diapers, bottles)?

Phase 3 - Contracts and Implantation

This section provides the recommended steps during the contracts and implantation phase as well as tips and tactics to ensure that you have recourse if you run into problems.

Step 1 – Setting up for Success

Start by hiring a surrogacy lawyer in the U.S. and a translator who is fluent in Spanish (or language of the surrogacy country) and proficient in English. Start with these two resources even if you plan to work with an agency in Mexico.

The lawyer is responsible for reviewing contracts with the translator or with the agency that will handle the surrogacy process. The lawyer can ensure that contracts include protections to address fraud, failure to perform, indemnification due to omissions, and a service guarantee. This is important because some active surrogacy facilitators are former Planet Hospital employees who have been disbarred from legal practice and others who are under investigation for fraud. Even if you have thoroughly vetted your providers, it's wise to have protections in the contract.

Step 2 – The Contracts

Now it's time to ensure that you have copies of all the contracts before you sign up with an agency or any service providers. We recommend requesting the following contracts for review:

- Facilitator and/or agency agreement
- IVF clinic agreement
- Delivery doctor agreement
- Pediatrician agreement, if not included with delivery doctor agreement
- Agreement with Mexican surrogacy attorney
- Gestational surrogacy agreement
- Hospital agreement

Request full disclosure of each provider's relationships with all third-party services they use. It's important to contract with people who understand they are working for you. If they are paid by other parties, there may be a conflict of interest. Insist on a list of affiliates as well as a list of former IPs who were paid for their endorsements.

For example, an IP who endorsed our first agency actually was an employee of that agency. She had not yet completed the surrogacy process. The agency was selected because of her endorsement and other endorsements on the agency website. However, it turned out that the agency had the same employees working under multiple websites and using multiple agency names. The sites were endorsing each other, so these were not independent endorsements. We discovered four different sites operated by and employing the same people.[18]

Had we been more careful when we negotiated with the first agency, we could have avoided a lot of expense and time out of the U.S. We also could have held the U.S. agency accountable for omitting and misrepresenting key facts.

Protect yourself by adding indemnification to ensure that the agency must pay the legal fees and additional costs of immigration if the agency or its affiliated service providers engage in fraudulent behaviors or, through their acts of omission, mislead you into doing something you otherwise would not have done. This will give you recourse in a U.S. court.

We also recommend adding an amicable termination clause with installment payments instead of making a full payment into an escrow account upfront. That positions you to terminate the contract early and minimizes the amount of money a shady agency is able to embezzle.

If you contract with an entity who works with only one doctor, hospital, agency, or IVF clinic, you're limited in your options based on what they have to offer. If the agency is in U.S., it will be able to enforce the terms of the agreement under U.S. laws. It may cost you a lot of money to get out of the contract if you decide their services are subpar.

---

[18] When we tried to post something on one of the sites regarding our negative experience, the owners blocked us and threatened to sue us and our surrogate. That's when we discovered that the agencies and sites were owned and operated by the same people.

57

Figure 12 summarizes some of the major activities you need to perform in this phase. This is not a comprehensive list but it worked for us during our journey. Feel free to add or delete items based on your unique needs.

Figure 12. Contract Activities

Retain surrogacy lawyer and/or in-country translator to review contracts.

Translate, review, negotiate, and revise all contracts/agreements.

Translate the surrogacy agreement back into Spanish.

Understand what you are signing.

Complete all contract-related health exams, including blood tests and viability of carrier (both IPs and the surrogate).

Execute agreements with the surrogate, the clinic/hospital, and other service providers prior to implantation.

Translation into English

Unless you are truly fluent in Spanish, have all contracts translated into English (or your native language, if it isn't English) so you can review them and understand exactly what you are signing. It's a time-consuming task because every service provider likely has its own contract that an attorney drew up with the best interest of the provider in mind.

Before you sign, ensure that all standard contract terms are included, that you understand the implications of every term, and that all appropriate protections have been incorporated. If you don't follow this advice, you're setting yourself up for problems.

Ability to Fulfill the Terms of the Agreement

Before you execute any agreements, complete all blood work and health examinations. This ensures that both the IPs and surrogate can fulfill their part of the agreement before, during, and after the pregnancy. They will also help you determine what services you will and will not need. Here are the key exams you need to take care of prior to signing any contract:

- Medical history for all parties

- Blood tests for IPs and surrogate to discover any factors that would prevent a healthy pregnancy; include testing the surrogate for STDs and anemia
- Viability test of sperm and/or eggs to increase the likelihood they will result in a positive pregnancy

Translation back into Spanish

The next step is to translate the updated gestational agreement and/or agency contracts, if applicable, back into Spanish, along with the IP birth certificates and passport information for the contract execution.

The translator should work as a mediator between you and your surrogate to finalize the gestational agreement.

Make Sure Everything Is in Writing

Negotiate everything up front — IVF, delivery, hospital, and attorney services — and make sure everything is in writing so you don't end up paying thousands of extra dollars because you relied on verbal promises.

For example, a family that exited in August of 2015 reported that the agency they had been working with hit them with an additional $6,500 in expenses because many of the items that were discussed did not end up in the contract. In another case, a couple contracted to pay a certain amount for the surrogate's travel expenses. It turned out that the surrogate lived nearby, and there were virtually no travel expenses. The IPs had to pay anyway.

In our case, a hospital and clinic staff member and a doctor tried to charge extra for items that were included in the contract. We didn't have to pay these fees because our translator spotted the duplicate charges and explained them to us.

Attorney

Be sure that your contract with the attorney in Mexico includes all fees, including registering the gestational agreement with the Tabasco courts, notary services, and drawing up of any additional documents or agreements required to get passports for your country. If you are using a lawyer to get the birth certificate from the Registro Civil, make sure to document which services are included and which are not.

IVF Clinic

Ask the IVF clinic to include a fee schedule in the contract. Key things to include in the agreement are medications, number of IVF attempts, embryo freezing (if that is an option), all lab tests (such as blood work for viability of sperm and eggs), and STD screenings. Our first agency in the U.S. led us to believe that lab work and medicines were included in our contract. The IVF doctor explained that they were not. You're more likely to get the right information if you go directly to the source.

Surrogacy Agency

If you use a surrogacy agency, take care to document everything and avoid any contract terms that could result in legal trouble. One couple told us they were charged for health insurance. Health insurance for a surrogate is not legal in Mexico. IPs must either pay for private medical services or use public services. Another couple was charged to freeze the embryos, but were told the contract included only one IVF attempt and that additional attempts would cost more.

If the agency is charging for a translator's services, ask for a detailed list of services that the translator will provide. And make sure the translator is proficient in English and Spanish. We spoke to translators at two agencies and they barely spoke English.

Hospital

The hospital contract should include quality-of-care clauses and specify costs for normal delivery, emergency care such as blood transfusions, neonatal intensive care, the ICU for the surrogate, additional costs for each multiple, pediatrician, anesthesiologist, and other medical charges. When the hospital office manager tried to charge us an extra $3,000, we were able to resolve the problem by pointing to the contract. Don't hesitate to ask for discounts during the negotiation process and, if the hospital agrees to them, make sure the discounted pricing is reflected in the final contract.

Surrogacy/Gestational Agreement

This can be a touchy area because some agencies have modeled their surrogacy/gestational contracts after those written in countries in which commercial surrogacy is legal. You need to be sure you understand what it takes for the agreement to be legal in the country the surrogacy is taking place. For example, for the agreement to be legal in Mexico, it has to follow specific rules:

- The agreement must be signed in Mexico. The Registro Civil checks *tramite* time stamps to confirm that travel dates match up with contract execution dates. Remember to take a picture of your tramite in case this comes up later.
- By law, the agreement must be in Spanish. American agency contracts and/or surrogacy agreements in English do not protect you under Mexican law and are not valid in Mexico unless they are executed in Mexico in Spanish and according to Mexican law.
- The contract must be signed *before* IVF takes place to secure parental rights from the moment of embryo creation in the IVF clinic.
- The contract cannot specify or contain any charges for health insurance for the surrogate. Beware of any agency that tries to charge you for this. IPs need to be prepared to pay for emergencies or complications before or during birth in Mexico.
- In line with the legal mandate for altruistic surrogacy, no formal agreement can contain terms that indicate the surrogate will profit from the contract or receive money other than expenses directly related to the surrogacy.

Here are some of the key terms to include in the agreement:

- Maximum number of IVF attempts
- Mutually agreed-upon termination clause for the contract or pregnancy (if you are comfortable with abortion)
- Length of time IPs will cover expenses
- Frequency and means of communication during IVF and pregnancy
- Number of embryos to be implanted per cycle
- Travel and expense requirements for the surrogate to give birth, attend the birth registration, and attend any official procedures to immigrate the baby in Mexico City

- Emergency considerations for childcare, travel, and/or caregiver in case of issues with the pregnancy in the last trimester or in the event of a miscarriage

Step 3 – Preparing for and Undergoing IVF

With all the contracts in place, you're ready for what is one of the most exciting parts of the whole surrogacy process. This is an amazing opportunity to build the IP/surrogate relationship.

The IVF doctor will talk to you, your partner, and your surrogate. This is not the time to try to save money by leaving out the translator. The doctor will discuss in detail medical information, the side effects of the drugs your surrogate and you will take to coordinate your menstrual cycles and prepare the surrogate's womb to receive the embryo. Figure 13 summarizes the activities that occur during this step.

It takes approximately six weeks to synchronize cycles. The procedures involve birth control pills for the synchronization followed by injections to stimulate ovaries to produce additional eggs. You don't have to be in Mexico the entire time. Much of it can take place in the U.S. You can get the birth control pills and the medication for stimulating your ovaries from your OB/GYN or from the IVF doctor in Mexico. WebMD and other reputable sites document the procedure and describe potential problems.

The surrogate must refrain from normal activity and stay in bed for the first few days after the implantation to ensure her chances of a successful pregnancy. We cannot stress enough how important it is that she have a partner or caregiver to assist her during this first part of the surrogacy process.

It takes about three weeks to tell if the IVF is successful. Your chances are about 50/50. We were all so impatient to find out if we were pregnant that Karla took a home pregnancy test about two weeks after implantation. It was positive. At three weeks, we did an ultrasound to identify how many gestational sacks took.

We were fortunate that both embryos took and our first ultrasound showed we were having twins. Everyone was thrilled at our luck getting pregnant on the first try.

Figure 13. Implantation Activities

Prepare womb and synchronize cycles between the surrogate and the egg provider.

Create embryos.

Implant the number of embryos agreed upon in the surrogacy contract.

Test for pregnancy.

If positive, celebrate, then move to next phase.

If negative repeat IVF cycle for as many attempts as specified in contract.

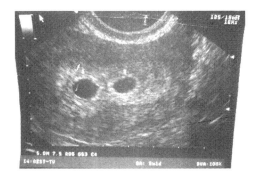

Phase 4 – Pregnancy and Planning for Delivery

Congratulations! You are officially pregnant. So now your job is to make sure that your surrogate and your child receive proper care. Supporting your surrogate, establishing emergency plans, finalizing travel plans, gathering all the documents you'll need in Mexico (or country of surrogacy) and getting your home ready for the baby are some of the activities in this phase.

During the First Trimester

Like any pregnant woman, the surrogate should have monthly checkups with an OB/GYN. Don't scrimp on medical care because regular checkups can uncover conditions early so they can be addressed before complications occur. In our case, Karla was diagnosed with a urinary tract infection and required special medications. She also developed anemia and required four blood transfusions. Without early diagnosis, our babies could have died or been mentally delayed and Karla's life could have been placed at risk.

IPs can participate in the routine checkups without traveling to Mexico. Karla streamed the ultrasounds using YouTube and Skype on her smartphone. We were able to talk to the doctor and understand what was going on in real time. It was like being there. We really loved the experience.

Figure 14 through Figure 19 summarize some of the major activities you'll complete during this phase.

Figure 14. First Trimester: Preparation for a Healthy Pregnancy

Set up regular office visits and checkups for your surrogate. If possible, attend via Skype, especially for major milestones such as ultrasounds.
Have the surrogate bring all previous medical records to the first visit.
Prepay office visits and communicate with your surrogate regularly to make sure she goes to all appointments.
If necessary, make arrangements for her transportation to the doctor's office.
Make sure the doctor includes initial tests for diabetes and anemia.

If you need a translator to help you communicate with the doctor or surrogate, be sure to include him or her in the call.

Provide prenatal vitamins, folic acid, and extra vitamin C and iron.

Request an additional round of blood tests early in the pregnancy to detect anemia if the surrogate is carrying multiples.

(Optional) Provide a little extra money for the surrogate to treat herself or her family — for example, to pick up dinner on a day when she is feeling tired or nauseous.

During the Second Trimester

The second trimester is the time to think about preparing the nursery, creating baby registries, and going to baby showers. It's also the time to establish contingency plans and prepare for the trip to Tabasco.

Figure 15. Second Trimester: Pregnancy and Planning Activities

Investigate and begin mapping out travel plans for your surrogate, including air travel, ground transportation, and so forth.

Investigate lodging for yourself and your surrogate, and create a contact list to use in Mexico.

Have birth certificates for IPs translated into Spanish so they are ready in case of early delivery.

Contact the U.S. embassy in Mexico City to sign up for the Step Program for Travel Alerts with State.gov and to obtain the list of documents required for your child's citizenship.

Confirm that your Mexican lawyer registered your gestational contracts with the Secretary General in Tabasco.

If inducing lactation, begin the process eight to twelve weeks prior if you are not using birth control to simulate a pregnancy, or six week prior if you are.

You should also make arrangements for someone to take care of things on the home front while you're out of the country for the birth, and have an emergency plan for early delivery. Figure 16 summarizes questions you should answer to create a contingency plan in case the baby arrives early.

Figure 16. Contingency Plan for Early Delivery

- Who will care for your home, pets, and/or children?
- Who will care for your surrogate and her family if she has medical issues that require bed rest?
- How will you handle unexpected infant medical issues?
- Have you identified someone to make decisions and handle your affairs at home while you are in Mexico?

Assemble a Required Documents

The same documents are required to obtain both the birth certificate from the Mexican government and citizenship papers from the U.S. government. You'll take some of the documents with you when you go to Mexico for the delivery. Others you'll obtain once you are in Mexico.

Start early because it takes time to gather all the documents you need, and the lead times for some can be lengthy. For example, we had to renew our sons' passports, a process that can take up to six weeks. Figure 17 lists the documents you'll pack before you leave the U.S.

Figure 18 lists the documents you will obtain in Mexico.

Figure 17. Documents to Pack Before You Leave the U.S.

- IPs' birth certificates
- Spanish translation of IPs' birth certificates notarized by a U.S. notary public
- U.S. passports for the IPs with stamped travel pages to Mexico for IVF and other reasons, along with pictures of *tramites* or entry documentation
- IPs' driver's licenses or photo IDs other than a passport
- IPs' marriage certificate
- Tax forms for previous five years for U.S. consulate (only two copies required)
- Proof of residency in U.S. for previous five years for U.S. consulate (only two copies required); acceptable proof includes high school/college degrees, social security statements, mortgage statements, and/or utility bills
- Permission to travel letters from each IP giving the other IP permission to travel with the child in Mexico (once the child is born)
- All medical receipts to prove the altruistic nature of the arrangement

- Original signed and notarized versions of the gestational agreement and all other contracts

Figure 18. Required Documents You Will Obtain in Mexico

- Copies of photo IDs for witnesses for contracts and birth certificate (Witnesses do not have to be at the consulate. You just need a copy of their photo IDs.)
- Letter from IVF and delivery doctors describing IVF, medical history, and delivery; the letter from IVF doctor must include date of conception; the letter from delivery doctor must include the delivery date, and IPs' relationship to child. These letters are typically created when the IVF doctor transfers the patient to the delivery doctor and after the delivery doctor has delivered the baby and prior to the baby's release from the hospital.)
- All medical records for the surrogacy from both the doctors (IVF, delivery, and pediatrician) and any donor agreements
- Medical records from the hospital such as the record of birth in the surrogate's name with footprints of the baby
- Keepsakes such as the medical ID bracelets from the hospital or signage to prove you were at the birth
- Ultrasound photos of the baby and photos of the mother at different stages of pregnancy to demonstrate the ongoing relationship and to prove no child trafficking occurred
- Record of child's immunization at the hospital or immediately after discharge
- Two copies of a letter from the Registro Civil to U.S. consulate citing the applicable civil code
- One photo for the SRE to go with the pediatrician's letter of health and another for the U.S. passport. The photo sizes are different for each document, so when you order the photos, specify you need one set for a U.S. passport and another for a Mexican passport. (Wal-Mart is a good place to get the photos.)

Except where otherwise indicated, you'll need the originals and eight copies of each documents:

- Two for the Secretary General
- Two for the Registro Civil
- Two for the U.S. consulate
- One extra in case one of the government entities loses a copy
- One to leave in the U.S. with a friend or family member in case you need to send it to a government body in the U.S.

Finalize Travel Plans – Two Months Prior to Birth

Finalize travel plans for you and your surrogate about two months prior to the birth. The surrogate needs to be in Villahermosa four to six weeks prior to the birth. With that in mind, it is best to start providing the surrogate's additional per diem and lodging for living in Villahermosa by month seven. Note: we have been told the new laws will require the surrogate to be a resident of the state of Tabasco in 2016. You may still need to pay for travel from her village or home to Villahermosa where most of the reputable IVF Clinics and Hospitals are.

Book the surrogate's travel to Villahermosa and her lodging. Be aware that sites such as www.airbnb.com or www.vrbo.com cater to expatriates. They often mark up the price for foreigners. You can save money on lodging by asking the translator or agency to find lodging on Mexican travel websites. We did this and paid the surrogate the funds in advance so she could pay in pesos which saved about $40 to $80 per day. Sometimes the delivery doctor or hospital will have discounts at nearby hotels or recommend economical accommodations. Another way to reduce the costs is to use your miles from credit cards or travel.

At this time, you should also contact the Mexican lawyer to confirm the contracts have been reviewed by the Secretary General and everything required for citizenship is in order. This includes any paperwork needed from your home country. Also select a DNA lab from the AABB accredited lab list and preorder DNA kits now or at beginning of the third trimester. (If you are not doing DNA testing due to blood transfusions or other issues, skip this step.)

Figure 19 offers suggestions for this final planning stage.

Figure 19. Plan for your Trip

Pack for at least a four- to five-week stay in Mexico. (See Appendix B for a list of what to pack.)

Have everything ready at 32 weeks in case of an early delivery.

Double check your required documents packet to make sure you have originals and copies of all paperwork.

Contact the delivery doctor and the hospital to finalize special requests and timing, including translation services, staying in a separate or the same room as surrogate, and breastfeeding.

We recommend waiting until month 8 to book your own flights because things can be unpredictable. Emergencies and early deliveries may require you to reschedule flights, which could result in change fees.

Because of Karla's anemia, she and Ian moved to Villahermosa at 31 weeks (about nine weeks prior to full term). Our daughters arrived four weeks and four days early so we were glad that the family had moved so early. For our part, we had to reschedule our flights several times.

As part of our final planning, we created a single document that listed all key information and helped us plan for total time and estimated expenses for our time in Mexico. We took a copy with us and left a copy with friends and family in the U.S. The document included the following key information:

- Calendar/agenda – cities, contacts, arrival/departure dates for each location, and addresses and phone numbers for hotels and other lodging
- Contacts – emergency contacts in Mexico and the U.S. for IPs; next of kin; caregiver for home, pets, and children; contact information for the delivery doctor, translator, surrogate, and U.S. and Mexican lawyers
- Air travel and ground transportation — contact numbers for airline and car rental companies along with confirmation numbers and discount codes
- IPs' cell phone numbers in Mexico

Figure 20 provides information on how long it takes to process various documents. Use the information to help you plan your itinerary. Keep in mind, however, that if your child is born near a holiday, most Mexican and U.S. government offices in Mexico will be closed. These office closures may extend

69

the time it takes to complete processing, so get a list of Mexican holidays from your provider or translator and factor in potential delays.

Figure 20. Timelines for Planning Your Stay in Mexico

Villahermosa

Item	Min/Max	Plan for	Notes
Mexican birth certificate	5 days minimum 5-10 days average	2 weeks+	same-sex couples should allow 10 days or more
Child's Mexican passport	2-4 months		Schedule appointment prior to birth at https://citas.sat.gob.mx/citasat/home.aspx. The assistance of a reputable attorney can ensure timely completion assuming there are no complications and you have all the necessary paperwork.

Mexico City

Item	Min/Max	Plan for	Notes
DNA testing	3-4 weeks	4 weeks	Can also be done in Tijuana
Consular Report of Birth Abroad (CRBA)	3-4 weeks	4 weeks	Concurrent with DNA testing
Child's U.S. passport	3-4 weeks	4 weeks	Can pay extra to expedite by processing with CRBA once DNA testing confirms genetic link
Social security number	2-4 months	4 months	This piece is optional. You can have it processed at the same time as CRBA/passport at the U.S. consulate or wait to visit a social security office in the U.S. It will be sent to your address in the U.S.

Final Details Before you Leave Home

Any time you leave home for an extended time, there are details that need to be taken care of in your absence. Arrange for a friend or family member to take responsibility for:

- Your home. Check the mail, pick up newspapers and packages left at the door, water plants, and ensure that the lawn is mowed and that a pool and other amenities are cared for.
- Pets. Have someone care for pets or optionally book a stay at a pet motel.
- Children. If have children in school and they cannot accompany you to Mexico, make arrangements for their care.

You might consider suspending delivery of mail and newspapers. And you should definitely contact your credit card companies to notify them of your temporary locations. This will help in case a credit card is lost or stolen.

If only one parent will be in Mexico during the four to six weeks after delivery, that parent must have a notarized letter from the other parent allowing the parent to travel with the child within Mexico. My husband and I prepared one for each other because we had to take turns spending time with the girls in Mexico and with our boys in the U.S.

Phase 5 - Delivery and Citizenship

With surrogacy, the most important thing IPs can do is expect the unexpected. Even the best planning goes out the window in an instant when it comes to a baby's or surrogate's health. Our daughters arrived 4-½ weeks earlier than expected. We had several business engagements booked. I was the headliner for a workshop in Boston and our sons were still in school. When we got the call, it was obvious that our plans didn't matter anymore. We had to do what was best for the babies. We packed up and headed to Mexico.

All the preplanning we had done made it easier to rearrange our plans. We knew what we had to do, we just had to do it sooner instead of later.

If you are rushed, don't forget to allow time to:

- Convert dollars to pesos — You can convert currency before you leave the U.S. at some AAA offices and at currency exchange offices in major cities. Or you can exchange currency at the airport in Mexico City during your layover to Villahermosa.
- Pack baby and personal items you'll need at the hospital
- Double check your required documents packet to make sure everything is there, and that you have the packet with you when you head to the airport
- Schedule any last minute wire transfers or PayPal payments to cover final charges for the hospital, delivery doctor, and surrogate. Schedule payments to arrive on the day after the scheduled birth.

Girls patiently waiting to be born on April 7, 2014.

Night before Delivery – Calm before the Storm

Your surrogacy agreement contains terms you've agreed upon — for example, natural delivery versus C-section. Sometimes plans change due to emergencies. If you followed the recommendations in the contracts section, the changes won't cause problems because you've included includes alternate courses of action in your surrogacy your agreement.

The night before delivery, take time to share your joy with the surrogate and her family. For us it was a time for the two families to focus on the culmination of our amazing journey. We all had a nice dinner together. We spent time confirming some final details with Karla:

- Did she still want me to be in the delivery room?
- Did she still want to provide breast milk? (Karla pumped so I could supplement my breastmilk.)
- Did she still want to share a room with me afterward delivery?
- Did she still want to hold the babies?

People have mixed feelings about issues like these and they can change their minds. Remember that the night before delivery can be a scary situation for the surrogate and she may want someone from her family present.

We strongly recommend that you also get snacks and sterile water packed and ready to take to the hospital. We took care of this on our way to the hospital the day of the delivery, and it took longer than we expected. Also, make sure you take a camera to the hospital.

The Big Day

On delivery day, arrive 30 minutes before the time the doctor has recommended so you will have time to settle in and to ask any last minute questions. If you and your surrogate have agreed that you will be in the delivery room, the experience will be an amazing and very moving one. You'll be impressed by the professionalism and quality of care provided by the medical team. The hospital where our twins were born was on par with such facilities as Stanford Medical Center where my husband had heart surgery.

Do what you can to help the surrogate through labor and delivery. I talked to Karla during labor to distract her from the pain. A big topic of conversation was what she wanted for our celebration dinner. She wanted shrimp.

We arrived at the hospital later than planned but fortunately we were there 20 minutes before our first daughter, Gabriella was born. Emma came along seven minutes later.

There was a pediatrician for each baby. They did a great job. Having given birth to my two sons, I can honestly say that Karla's experience was just as good and, in some cases, better than what my husband and I experienced in the U.S. I was there when they assessed the overall health scores, so I knew right away that our daughters were fine. The doctors took them to a separate room with incubators and facilities to care for them until all health indicators checked out.

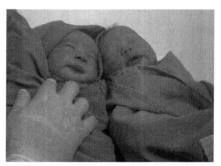

Girls just after birth on April 8, 2014

After the Birth

We imagine that the "after the birth" experience is unique for every couple. In our case, we were whisked away to the room assigned to our family. It was right across from the ICU where the babies were kept because of their very small size — just over four pounds.

We learned that a big difference between the U.S. and Mexico is that you don't get as many marketing samples in Mexican hospitals. So mark all your supplies with your name and bring them to the hospital — bottles, breast milk, clothing for the surrogate and the child, baby blankets, diapers, and so forth.

We were glad we had our own translator, Ian, in the room. We had developed a relationship with Ian from the beginning. Having a baby is a very personal experience and the relationship with Ian was critical because we were more at ease with him in the room than we would have been with a stranger.

Although the hospital had translation services, they were not always available when the doctors came by to check on the babies or on Karla. Although I speak Spanish, it was comforting that Ian was able to help ask the nurses specifics around medical terminology. For example, when I was asking for a wipe to clean my daughter's backside, the nurse handed me a maxi-pad. We all had a good laugh and Ian was able to have them bring additional wet wipes.

Ian helped with so many things, including scheduling appointments with the pediatricians and getting directions to their office where, two days after birth, the girls received all immunizations required for the birth certificates.

Documents You Need from the Hospital

You need to obtain several documents from the hospital and the doctors because they will be required by the Registro Civil, the U.S. embassy, and the SRE. The time at the hospital can be crazy, especially with multiples. So pull out your checklist from time to time and make sure you don't forget to get these documents. When you receive them, double check the accuracy of the dates and all other information.

- Travel letter for baby – Getting the passport at the U.S. embassy requires a plane trip to Mexico City. However, airlines do not allow a child to fly in the first nine to 30 days after birth without a letter from a pediatrician. So make sure you ask the pediatrician to provide a letter authorizing travel.
- Hospital records – The Mexican hospital will provide a birth record in the surrogate's name, with her fingerprints and the baby's footprint. This record is critical and required for the birth registry (to get the birth certificate), Consular Report of Birth Abroad, and passports.

- Letters from delivery doctor and pediatrician – You will need a letter from both the delivery doctor and the pediatrician. The delivery doctor's letter confirms his or her understanding of the IPs, confirmation of the pregnancy, delivery, and health of the surrogate. The pediatrician's letter confirms immunizations and health.
- Receipts – Take receipts of all medical procedures and payments you made to the delivery doctor, pediatrician, and hospital. These documents help with the birth certificates, CRBA, and passports as well as with your taxes. (Ask your accountant what you can write off and need documentation to prove.)

Check for Clerical Errors

Although we loved our doctor and lawyer, we did have a few issues with their business manager. On multiple occasions, the bills she provided had overcharges. On some occasions she told us she didn't receive a payment from the bank and asked us to pay her in cash. Each time we had to escalate the issue to the doctor. She suggested that the reason for the mistakes or oversights was my limited proficiency in Spanish.

Ian was extremely helpful here. He checked the bill and found another duplicate charge. He told her she had to stick to the agreement and not charge extra "gringo" rates. In our excitement over our new babies, we might have missed this and paid the duplicate charge.

Overbilling, double charging, and errors in paperwork occur in the U.S. as well, so checking and rechecking are always important. Having a translator who worked directly for us was, in our opinion, a major factor in successfully navigating the surrogacy process.

Getting the Birth Certificate

For children born of surrogacy in the U.S., the birth certificates are typically issued at the hospital. The parents named on the birth certificate are the woman who gives birth (the surrogate) and the intended father. The step-parent adoption process enables IPs to change the mother's name to the intended mother. The adoption process involves having the surrogate abdicate her rights to the child in front of a judge. Once that process is complete, a new birth certificate is issued. For more information on this process, consult a surrogacy and/or adoption attorney in the state in the U.S where the adoption will take place.

For a child born in Mexico, the Registro Civil in Villahermosa processes the paperwork and issues the birth certificate. The process for getting the birth certificate under a surrogacy agreement is straightforward and typically takes two meetings over a period of 10 to 15 days. Input provided by several IPs indicates that it takes a little longer for same-sex couples than heterosexual couples.

For us, the process took only two days. It appears that delays experienced by some IPs were the result of mistakes made by providers they had hired. For example, a San Francisco couple claimed to be stuck in Mexico because the Mexican government had placed a hold on all birth certificates for U.S. citizens. That was incorrect. The real problem was that their lawyer failed to follow the proper process. We referred the IPs to another lawyer who knew the process and they received their birth certificate within one day.

Review the "Legal and Regulatory Issues" section to make sure you understand the laws and the "Assemble the Required Documents" section to make sure you have all the right documents with you.

Take pesos (or local currency) with you to make additional copies. They may have a copier on site or you can ask the staff at the Registro whom they would recommend for additional copies.

This process can be as smooth or as complicated as you make it. From our experience and feedback from others that used our checklist, this is what we recommend:

Preregister with the Secretary General

You can shorten the time it takes to get birth certificates by having the deputy director of the secretary general for the State of Tabasco review your contracts and supporting evidence before delivery. This review, which takes a couple of days, confirms that the laws of Mexico were followed and the type of surrogacy is recorded. Your translator, lawyer, or agency can handle this.

Step 2 – Get Birth Certificate from the Registro Civil –
http://www.registrosciviles.org/formulario-nacimiento

It is the Registro Civil in Tabasco that provides the birth certificates. Copies of the birth certificates are inexpensive — less than $5. It is, however, an all-day process. Delegado[19] de La Rosa, who is in charge of the Registro Civil in Tabasco, is a formal but delightful person who follows the letter of the law. He made it clear that the service is free of charge for everyone, including citizens and foreigners, and the only requirement is that you obey the law.

Our surrogate, her fiancé, our girls, and me at the Registro Civil waiting for our interview.

The Registro Civil in Tabasco randomly flags IPs for interviews to confirm that everything is legal. The interview includes everyone involved in the surrogacy relationship: the IPs, the surrogate, and her family. Our takeaway from the interview is that Mexican officials want to ensure that no one is taken advantage of as a result of the arrangement — not the surrogate, not the IPs, not the child born.

The general process for obtaining the Mexican birth certificate is:

---

[19] Delegado is the title used for the person overseeing a government office and is similar to representative or chief executive in English. Each government office has a delegado.

1) Have your lawyer or translator preregister with the Registro Civil a couple of weeks prior to birth and confirm the procedure to follow. This eliminates surprises, costs, and delays resulting from legal or procedural changes.

2) During the review process, ask for approval for you to go through the normal process, assuming there are no issues with your case. Request a pre-approval letter to reduce the wait time on the day you go in for the birth certificate.

3) The morning of the appointment, one of you should arrive at 6:00 am to get a spot in line because there are a limited number of appointments. The hours are from 8:30 to 3:00. Plan to spend the entire day. There's no air conditioning in the waiting room, so bring drinks and things to keep you and the baby comfortable.

4) The clerk at the window will ask for your paperwork one document at a time. Provide each document as it is requested. Be patient. This takes time and trying to rush things may cause the clerk to delay your process.

5) If your case is flagged for any reason, the delegado will meet with you to review the paperwork and speak to all parties. Our case was flagged because we were one of the first foreign parents. Because our surrogate and her fiancé were with us, the delegado was reassured.

6) At the end of the meeting, request a letter for the U.S. consulate stating that you have complied with all Mexican laws. You need at least three originals: two for the consulate and one for your files.

7) Once your case is approved, a clerk will sit with you and type the birth record. Be prepared to answer questions about your history, your parents' names and dates of birth, and other data found on a birth certificate.

8) You must order copies of the birth certificate at the Registro Civil's outside window and pay for them. We recommend getting three to four copies to have one for the SRE for the Mexican passport, one for the U.S. consulate for the U.S. passport, and two for your files.

9) The birth certificate is typically ready in three to 15 days.

Phase 6 – Exit (U.S. Citizenship and Mexican Passports)

You've finally reached the final step, which is obtaining your child's U.S. citizenship, U.S. passport, and Mexican passport.

Citizenship

Children born in the U.S. are automatically U.S. citizens, regardless of the citizenship of the woman giving birth. So if your surrogate is a Mexican citizen but gives birth to your child in the U.S., you can skip the citizenship steps.

This section presents the general process for obtaining U.S. citizenship for a child born of a surrogate in Mexico. The process is similar for children born in India and Thailand. If you are working with a surrogate in India, Nepal, or other country, you need to educate yourself thoroughly on the surrogacy laws of that country and be aware of any restrictions resulting from The Hague Convention on Intercountry Adoptions.

Figure 21 summarizes the steps for easy reference.

Steps to Citizenship

As IPs from the U.S., your best bet is to conduct the entire citizenship process through the U.S. embassy in Mexico City. This section provides details on the process.

Step 1

Review the manual governing American citizen services related to conveying U.S. citizenship so you know what to expect.[20] The better educated you are with respect to the laws, the less likely it is you will experience delays.

---

[20] The manual specifically states to flag cases of older parents in heterosexual relationships, especially if the woman is near or beyond child-bearing age. If this is your situation, you may face challenges in processing your case. See http://www.state.gov/documents/organization/86757.pdf

Step 2

Make an appointment and obtain the form for procuring the Consular Report of Birth Abroad (CRBA) form, passport, and DNA testing (if needed). You can do this online at http://evisaforms.state.gov/ACSSchedulingSystem.asp.

When you schedule the appointment, ask the embassy staff the cost of processing the forms so you know how much money to take with you. We suggest cash (pesos) because the ATM/credit card machine isn't always reliable.

Pack supplies and plan ahead for your interview as this process could take anywhere from a few hours up to the entire day. IPs are permitted to bring diapers and bottles of formula. However, you or the baby will be required to drink some formula in front of embassy personnel to demonstrate that the bottles do not contain explosives. You cannot bring electronic devices such as cell phones or computers, so leave them at your hotel or apartment.

Complete the CRBA form in black ink prior to going to the embassy. Confirm that all documentation is complete and that you have passport photos.

Arrive at the embassy early. You must show your U.S. passport to confirm your appointment. It takes time to clear security, so be patient. If you have your cell phone with you, they will put it in a plastic bag and keep it. You must retrieve it later. You are allowed only one diaper bag with formula and diapers. You may want to pack a snack in the diaper bag as well. You will be escorted to American Citizen Services to process your paperwork.

You need to check in at the window. There are two rooms, one for the general population and one for families. We suggest you wait in the room for families. It is generally quieter and easier for the baby to nap.

The staff will give you updates on how long it will take. You must pay for the CRBA processing, passports, and any other items you are requesting. They will call you in for your interview. During the interview they will review your paperwork and ask general questions about the surrogacy. Once you complete the interview process they will give you more information on their decisions and next steps.

If you are taking a DNA test, make sure you or your partner do not eat for two hours prior and the baby does not eat for one hour prior. You or your spouse should remain in the room at all times with the baby during the test. Confirm that the person collecting the sample follows the U.S. laws and proper procedures so the test will be valid.

Figure 21. Summary of the Steps to U.S. Citizenship

1. Complete the application for the Consular Report of Birth Abroad. The form is available at http://www.state.gov/documents/organization/156216.pdf
2. Schedule an appointment for an interview with U.S. embassy one month in advance of expected delivery
3. If you decide to submit to a DNA test, select the AABB lab from list found at http://www.aabb.org/sa/facilities/Pages/RTestAccrFac.aspx, pay for the testing kit, and have it sent to the embassy. The test sample must be taken at the embassy unless the consulate gives you permission to take it at the lab in the U.S.
4. Schedule the DNA test with the citizenship interview when you call the embassy in Mexico City at the same time. Ideally the same day or in close proximity.
5. To comply with the Immigration and Naturalization Act Sections 301 and/or 309, you have to provide the documentation listed below at the time of your interview. Further details are available at http://www.uscis.gov/us-citizenship/citizenship-through-parents

- Gestational agreement
- Hospital records
- Letters from doctors
- Letter from Registro Civil (optional)
- Proof of parent(s) U.S. citizenship (passport, utility bills, U.S. driver's license, birth certificates of parents) and residency for five years
- Proof of marriage for married couples if both names will be listed on the CRBA (marriage certificate)

Couples who use donor eggs or sperm can request to have both U.S. IPs listed on the Consular Report of Birth Abroad as long as both are the legal parents of the child in Mexico.

DNA, Anemia, and Your Legal Rights

DNA testing to establish a genetic link between the IPs and the child is not required by U.S. law. However, consulate and/or embassy personnel may request and even insist on testing before granting citizenship to the child. It is important that you know your rights.

If you agree to testing, you need to understand the factors that can result in a false negative reading, indicating that neither IP has a genetic link to the child. Those factors are:

- Improper handling of the swabs — People who aren't properly trained may make mistakes in collecting the sample and, as a result, introduce contaminants that cause an incorrect DNA reading.
- Food particles and their proteins in the mouth — This can occur if the person tested eats within two hours of having the sample taken, or is ill and vomits.
- Accidental switching of samples — This rarely happens, but can occur at the point of sample collection or at the lab.
- Blood transfusions — Transfusions are more prevalent in countries that have a higher incidence of anemia during pregnancy, and the higher incidence of multiples due to the IVF process that initiates the pregnancy.

Our experience with DNA testing did not go smoothly. We are sharing it here to illustrate the impact it can have on obtaining U.S. citizenship. We also have some also have some recommendations to help you avoid complications.

Our case involved at least two of the factors listed above. Despite our doctors' and our surrogate's best efforts to maintain a high iron count, Karla developed severe anemia primarily because she was carrying twins and had four blood transfusions, the last of which occurred just before delivery.

Moreover, mistakes were made when our babies underwent DNA testing at the U.S. embassy in Mexico City. One of our daughters was ill and was vomiting just before sample collection. This likely resulted in contaminants that could have caused a misreading.

This false negative caused a lot of trauma, expense, and delay. Ultimately, we had to apply for and obtain a humanitarian parole to reunite our family in the U.S. We also had to agree to a step-parent adoption of our daughter in an Arizona court even though the second DNA test for her was positive to clear the discrepancy in our file.

Had we been more knowledgeable about the factors that can cause an incorrect DNA test reading and about the law regarding DNA testing, we would have declined to do the testing until a later date, or refused altogether. Here's what you need to know: DNA testing is not a legal requirement for obtaining U.S. citizenship for your child.

Consulate and embassy personnel can suggest a DNA test, but they cannot require it. The Mexican birth certificate is sufficient evidence of your parental rights. The agreements with the surrogate, the IVF clinic/doctors, and others provide additional evidence of the biological link. Ask to have citizenship granted based on that evidence.

If you do agree to DNA testing, you have a right to select any approved AABB-accredited lab from the list the officials provide. The embassy cannot select the lab for you.

Exception Options - Humanitarian Parole

If the embassy continues to pressure you to get a DNA test and you are concerned due to a recent blood transfusion for the baby or surrogate, you can file for a humanitarian parole, which will allow you to take the child to the U.S. and pursue citizenship through the U.S. Customs and Immigration Services. The key is to apply before you establish your legal claim to citizenship.

To apply for humanitarian parole, go to http://www.uscis.gov/humanitarian/humanitarian-parole to review the eligibility requirements. You need to complete two forms. Form 131 is the request for parole. Read the instructions and provide supporting information for your request such as medical records for the blood transfusions or other justifications as to why it taking the DNA test is not currently a viable option.

If at any time you believe you are not receiving due process under the 14th amendment of the U.S. Constitution, go for a humanitarian parole, get back the to the U.S., and then file a complaint with the Office of Inspector General when you return to the U.S. Humanitarian paroles typically take about 30 days to process.

Getting your Child's Mexican Passport

Children born in Mexico are automatically granted Mexican citizenship under the Mexican Constitution. Similar to the U.S. government, the Mexican government requires that their citizens traveling to and from the country have a Mexican passport.

The passport is obtained from the SRE. We recommend that a translator accompany you to avoid confusion and frustration.

Our experience with the SRE in Merida was simple and straightforward. Apparently, however, several IPs have violated Mexican law during their surrogacy process. As a result, the SRE is now being extra cautious and the process is taking longer. The SRE will likely review all the documentation you provided to the U.S. embassy to ensure compliance with all applicable federal child trafficking laws and state surrogacy laws. The staff also ensures there has been no coercion and that the IPs and the child will reside in the IPs' home country.

Check with the SRE to understand how long it will take to process the paperwork and issue the passport. If the SRE has concerns about your case, it could take months. It may be easier to return to the U.S. and visit the local Mexican embassy to obtain the passport for your child.

All the forms are in Spanish, so it's helpful to have a translator assist with filling them out correctly. The forms are the same whether you are completing the process in Mexico or at a Mexican embassy in the U.S. As with any other government agency, the SRE wants everything completed accurately and completely in black ink. We learned the hard way that no other color will be accepted.

There are two forms you must download and complete[21]: OP5 (general application) and Form OP7. Form OP7 must be completed and notarized by the Mexican embassy in your home country if only one parent will be present during the processing of the passports.

Once you have completed the forms, go to one of the approved banks, complete the requisition form, and pay the fee for processing the passport. The SRE does not accept checks. The banks typically prefer pesos but will accept local currency. When we went through the process, it cost about 500 pesos per application. The list of banks and sample applications are available on the SRE website.[22]

You should have obtained passport photos in the sizes specified for both Mexican and U.S. passports. You'll need six photos for the Mexican passport and the pediatrician's letter, and a few extras just in case.

You'll need to visit your pediatrician for a letter of health. This is not the same letter you needed for the U.S. Department of State to obtain the birth records. It is a specific form letter that the pediatrician completes and keeps on file for the baby. The doctor needs two Mexican passport photos. One photo is pasted in the upper left corner of the letter with the pediatrician's official stamp to prove that he or she is validating the identity of the child. The letter includes a description of the child's general health and immunization records and approval for the child to travel. Mexican pediatricians are familiar with the form letter and provide it once you show them the receipt for passport. When you schedule the pediatrician appointment, explain that the purpose is to get the letter.

The next step is to schedule your appointment using the internet scheduling system for the SRE (https://citas.sre.gob.mx). You may need your translator's help to schedule the appointment. The appointments are in the child's name, so if you have multiples, schedule an appointment for each child.

On the day of your appointment:

---

[21] Forms are available at http://sre.gob.mx/

[22]

http://www.sat.gob.mx/terceros_autorizados/bancos_autorizados/Paginas/bancos_internet_vbancaria_ecinco.aspx

- Double check to be sure you have all documents including two copies of your Mexican passport receipts, the birth certificate, pediatrician's letter of health, Mexican passport photos, Form OP5, and, if needed, Form OP7.
- Arrive at least 15 minutes in advance to ensure you do not lose your appointment. Bring your translator with you as the SRE does not always have one available.
- The SRE will check all paperwork when you arrive. It if is not in order, you will have to leave, correct the problem, and reschedule.

The delays in the Mexican passports mentioned earlier have been caused by IPs who did not follow Mexican law because they or their agencies made mistakes in the process. The top reasons for delays are:

- **Surrogacy is illegal in country of the intended parents**. The SRE wants to ensure they are not allowing an illegal adoption or child trafficking to go unchecked. To avoid this, you should have consulted an immigration attorney in your country about how you legally immigrate a child.

- **Contracts were not executed according to Mexican law**. In several cases, IPs unknowingly followed bad advice from an agency. The biggest mistakes I have seen are contracts that were signed in the U.S. and the IPs do not have the tramite to prove the process was overseen by a notary and witness well versed in Mexican law. This includes contracts that were drafted by U.S. agencies that did not follow gestational agreement laws, contracts that were in English, and contracts that were not signed and notarized prior to implantation and/or birth.

- **Procedures that did not follow Mexican law or the law of the IPs' birth country**. In virtually every case we've seen in which the IPs had difficulties, the root cause was a failure to follow Mexican laws or the laws of the IPs' country. Examples include invalid surrogacy contracts, birth certificates issued in a format that doesn't meet the requirements of the IPs' country, and traveling with the child before he or she is deemed fit to travel by a Mexican medical professional.

Learn More

We recommend that you use this book for its intended purpose: as a guide for U.S. IPs going through surrogacy in Mexico. The surrogacy laws and processes are always evolving so it is important that you do your homework.

We try to follow changes in the laws, processes, and market but cannot guarantee that we always have the latest information. We do post updates to our Facebook page, Surrogacy in Mexico – Debunking Facts from Fiction. We also respond to emails at surrogacyfacts@gmail.com.

We welcome your feedback, requests for referrals, and inquiries for assistance. We often help IPs during the beginning of the process or toward the end if they are stuck and require additional information. We are not a facilitator or agency nor do we receive any commissions or referral fees.

Our only goal is to ensure that other IPs have the information they need to make informed decisions and, if they did not, to assist them in picking up the pieces and connecting them with seasoned professionals who are ethical, provide good service, and put the needs of the baby, IPs, and surrogate above their own profits.

There is too much corruption and unethical practice in surrogacy. We hope that in some small way we can give back by providing information for the IPs, surrogates and others to know what to avoid and what works when embarking on their surrogacy journeys.

Appendix A – Laws and Citizenship

Surrogacy Laws (Mexico)

We are not lawyers, but we do have a deep background in compliance and understanding legal applications of services and products. The information in this section is from the Código Civil of Tabasco that was translated for our case from our Mexican attorney, Cristina Valdez of La Cigüeña del Bebé.

To minimize complications and confusion avoid the following:

- Traditional surrogacy, which involves the surrogate donating genetic material. Otherwise you will have to adopt the child under the Hague Convention. If you are not a Mexican citizen, you cannot adopt a Mexican child under the age of five
- Embryo adoption or any situation in which both eggs and sperm are donated
- Implantation without proper the first executing a notarized gestational agreement in a Mexican court
- Creation of embryos or implantation at any clinic that cannot provide a Mexican COFEPRIS permit
- Commercial surrogacy
- Viewing pictures of egg or sperm donors

Tabasco Laws (Translated into English)

The State of Tabasco is the only Mexican state in which surrogacy is legal. State officials are considering changing the laws by the end of 2015 due to facilitators not following Mexican Law and poor treatment of surrogates. What those changes are and how they are going to be implemented is still unknown. Tabasco has been open to all genders and couples in general.

There are two legal codes that make a gestational substitute surrogacy a viable option in Tabasco. They are Article 92 and Article 347. The applicable codes in

Spanish. We've included English translations of key provisions provided by Cristina Valdez.

MARCO LEGAL PARA GESTACIÓN SUSTITUTA EN EL ESTADO DE TABASCO, MÉXICO

LEGAL FRAMEWORK FOR GESTATIONAL SURROGACY IN TABASCO, MEXICO
TABASCO CIVIL CODE
Article 92.

This section covers the recognition of motherhood for mothers of children born through a gestational substitute.

ARTICULO 92.- Deber de reconocer al hijo tanto la madre como el padre, que no estuvieren casados entre sí, tienen el deber de reconocer a su hijo; pero si no cumplen con este deber voluntariamente, no se asentará en el acta de nacimiento el nombre de los mismos y simplemente, se anotará la hora, día, mes año y lugar del nacimiento, así como el nombre propio y apellidos que se pongan a la persona cuyo nacimiento sea registrado. Si el padre o la madre o ambos piden por sí o por apoderado que en el acta de nacimiento se asiente su nombre, se hará constar éste y se mencionará en su caso la petición que en este sentido hagan el padre, la madre, o ambos, o el apoderado. Cuando el hijo sea presentado por uno de los progenitores, se asentará únicamente el nombre del que lo presente.

En el acta de nacimiento no se hará ninguna mención que califique la filiación en forma alguna. Las palabras "hijo legítimo", " hijo natural", "hijo ilegítimo", " hijo de padres desconocidos", "hijo de padre desconocido ", "hijo de madre desconocida", o " habido como consecuencia de cualquier método de reproducción humana artifical ", que se inserten con infracción de este artículo, se testarán de oficio, de manera que queden ilegibles. El Oficial del Registro Civil que inserte en el acta alguna de estas menciones será sancionado, la primera vez con una multa por el equivalente a quince días de salario mínimo general vigente en la Entidad y la segunda con destitución del cargo. La investigación de la paternidad y de la maternidad está permitida en los términos establecidos por este Código.

En el caso de los hijos nacidos como resultado de la participación de una madre gestante sustituta, se presumirá la maternidad de la madre contratante que la presenta, ya que este hecho implica su aceptación. En los casos en los que participe una madre subrogada, deberá estarse a lo ordenado para la adopción plena.

Se entiende por madre gestante sustituta, la mujer que lleva el embarazo a término y proporciona el componente para la gestación, más no el componente genético. Por el contrario, la madre subrogada provee ambos: el material genético y el gestante para la reproducción. Se considera madre contratante a la mujer que convenga en utilizar los servicios de la madre gestante sustituta o de la madre subrogada, según sea el caso.

Salvo el caso de que se trate de un hijo nacido de una madre gestante sustituta, cuando el hijo nazca de una mujer casada que viva con su esposo, el Oficial del Registro Civil no podrá asentar como padre a otro que no sea el mismo marido, excepto que éste haya desconocido al hijo y exista sentencia ejecutoria que así lo declare.

Translation and interpretation of highlighted text

In the case of children born as a result of gestational substitution, maternity will be presumed by the contracting mother as the contract in fact implies the acceptance of motherhood, whether she provides the genetic material or not. In the case in which a surrogate mother (provides genetic material and carries the child) full adoption will be in order.

Article 347 covers the legal rights of the intended mother to be the legal mother of the child whether or not she provided genetic material or not. This is only if the gestational substitute does not provide any genetic material.

CAPITULO IV
DE LAS PRUEBAS DE FILIACIÓN DE LOS HIJOS CUYOS PADRES NO FUEREN CÓNYUGES

ARTÍCULO 346.- En relación a la madre La filiación de los hijos cuyos padres no fueren cónyuges resulta con relación a la madre, del solo hecho del nacimiento. Para justificar este hecho, son admisibles todos los medios de prueba, y en los juicios de intestado o de alimentos se justificará la filiación respecto de la madre dentro del mismo procedimiento.

ARTÍCULO 347.- Respecto del padre Respecto del padre, la filiación se establece por el reconocimiento voluntario o por una sentencia que declare la paternidad; pero en el caso de concubinato se podrá justificar la filiación respecto del padre en el mismo juicio de intestado o de alimentos y será suficiente probar los hechos a que se refieren los artículos 340 y 372, tanto en vida de los padres como después de su muerte. Esta acción es imprescriptible y transmisible por herencia.

Sin embargo, como una excepción a esta presunción, cuando en el proceso reproductivo participe una segunda mujer, se presumirá madre legal a la mujer que contrata, ya sea que esta última provea o no el óvulo. Esto es, cuando la madre sustituta no es la madre biológica del niño nacido como resultado de una transferencia de embrión, la madre contratante deberá ser considerada la madre legal del niño y éste será considerado hijo legítimo de la mujer que contrató.

Translation and interpretation of highlighted text

However, when in the reproductive process a second woman participates, the contracting mother will be presumed the legal mother, whether she provided an egg or not. That is, when the gestational surrogate is not the biological mother of the baby born as a result of the embryo transplant, the contracting mother will be considered legal mother of the child and the legal child of the contracting mother.

The exact text in Spanish is available at:
http://www.icnl.org/.../.../Mexico/Tabasco_Codigo_Civil_2011.pdf

These laws are subject to change at any time. It is up to the IPs to keep track of any changes to surrogacy laws in the country where they are executing the surrogacy agreement.

Appendix B – Packing List for Abroad

The time is near and now you need to pack for your trip. Airline restrictions make it hard to bring more than two carry-on bags and one bag that you check. When you are expecting a baby this really puts a kink in things. In our case we had to prepare to pack for twins. This appendix was created to provide a good checklist of what you should plan to bring with you on your journey and what items are readily available in Mexico for you to pick up. What makes it complicated is that although you are allowed another bag for the baby and typically at least a car seat or stroller on the way home – this is not the case on the way to Mexico because you do not have the baby yet. All the items we mention below were fit into 2 large duffle bags and 4 carry-on bags with few exceptions. Note we did it for twins (double of everything).

You will want to bring enough for at least six weeks:

Item	Description/Notes
2 large duffle bags	Available at Costco, Target, and other places. Should be big enough to hold a portable crib, car seat, formula, diapers, and other key items.
Portable crib and 4 sets of sheets	We used a pillow to make ours softer and both of our twins fit in one crib.
Infant car seat	The carriers are great for taking the babies out and about. Models are available for twins.
Diapers	A newborn uses 8-10 diapers a day. Take enough for 2 weeks so you have time to focus on baby instead of shopping.
Baby wipes	Wipes in Mexico are thinner, so bring lots of wipe with you.
Mosquito netting	If you in Mexico during the summer, a mosquito net for the crib

for crib	keeps the baby safe from bites without insect repellents.
Calamine Lotion	This is difficult to find in Mexico, so take it with you.
Bottle warmer	1) **Bottle warmer** – Available at Target, Wal-Mart and other stores in the U.S. for about $20. 2) **Lots of bottles and bottle inserts** — Mexican hospitals do not provide bottles for newborns, and you may not be able to find your preferred brand in Mexico. 3) **Anti-bacterial dish soap** — We could not find anti-bacterial dish soap in Mexico, so bring enough to clean bottles and nipples.
Lots of bottles and bottle inserts	Mexican hospitals do not provide bottles for newborns, and you may not be able to find your preferred brand.
Anti-bacterial dish soap	We could not find anti-bacterial dish soap in Mexico, so bring enough to clean bottles and nipples.
Breast pump(s)	This is optional, in case you or the surrogate plans to breast feed. The pumps are cheaper in the U.S.
Infant formula	Most Mexican women breast feed. As a result, formula is pricey and, in our opinion, the quality isn't as good as what we found in the U.S. Even if you breast feed, supplemental formula is a good thing to have on hand. If you must buy formula in Mexico, SMA Gold and BIBO are
Pacifiers	You may want to bring pacifiers and a pacifier holder that snaps on to the baby's clothes. If you are breastfeeding and need orthodontic nipples, they are hard to find.
Lots of blankets and clothes	The hospital will expect you to have your own diapers, baby clothing, and blankets so have all these items in a diaper bag for easy transportation to the hospital.
Baby Toiletries	The baby will need toiletries immediately at birth. Bring 2 to 3 wash cloths, baby shampoo, infant Tylenol, nail clippers, mitts to cover the baby's hands to prevent scratching of the face, medicine dropper, digital thermometer, and teething ring.

Alcohol, gauze and Q-Tips	These items are for putting on the umbilical cord. They are available at Mexican pharmacies, but it's easier to take a small bottle of alcohol and a few swabs so you don't have to shop.
Coffee and powdered creamer	If you love your coffee, take it with you in case you don't like the coffee in Mexico.
Instant oatmeal	With newborns, it isn't always easy to get out of the room. Instant oatmeal, microwavable soups, and other quick meals are a godsend at these times.
Spanish dictionary for Medical Terms + Google Translate on Smart Phone	If you have a good translator this one will not be needed. We did have Google Translate on our smart phones but it is not always accurate. It is still better to have it than not to.
Skype/Voyage	Add these apps to your smartphone and/or laptops to save money on calls to the U.S. An alternative is to add international dialing to your cellphone calling plan. However, this route is more expensive.
Mexican cellphone	We called our local cellular providers and had them unlock our smartphones. We picked up a SIM card at the local OXXO for Telcel and would recharge it there. Having the smart phone was the smartest thing we could do because we used it for everything from communicating with one another to finding our way around in a foreign place. Google Maps worked the best for us in Mexico versus the other programs.
GPS app for your phone	Download the app to your smartphone before you go to Mexico to minimize download charges and ensure you have the English version.
Books, magazines, DVDs, and music	You'll be glad you have these when the baby is sleeping and you have a little downtime. Load up your Kindle, MP-3 player, DVD Player, and/or Laptop with entertainment.
IPs clothing and toiletries	Bring lightweight, comfortable clothing. Use local laundry services, which are less expensive than the hotel laundry service. (We spent about $2.00 a day.) (not at hotel but local one) is very cheap. We paid about $2 per day. Bring enough shampoo, conditioner, toothpaste, razors, and so forth, and then buy more at a store such as Walmart.

Appendix C — Considerations for Multiples

Start shopping early for some items if you are expecting multiples. It is important to note that the equipment is sometimes harder to find and not all of the items frankly are worth the additional costs. We found that basic items can cost as much to 2 ½ times more but they not provide the value. We thought we would add items we found useful during our stay in Mexico and after for our twin daughters.

- Weego – www.weego.com This carrier is best for when they are little. Once they hit about 15 pounds it gets a bit much to carry the two front facing. There are other carriers for two but we found it best to just get a single Bjorn for each. This was handy in doing basic household chores like vacuuming. The infant carriers worked well with a stroller back home.

- **Stroller** – although not recommended for Mexico – it is a must for the United States. These can range anywhere from $350 to $1500. You will only use them for a couple of years and not get your monies worth on the more expensive ones. We found a BabyTrend combo that had the infant car seats and stroller. Under $500 for the 2 car seats and stroller – still works great. We liked the inline stroller because the side by side is harder to get into doorways and manipulate in malls and other areas.

- **Infant Car Seats** – 2 singletons work just fine or a combination solution like above.

- **Pack-N-Play Crib** - Ditch the twin versions – we had one and returned it for a singleton. Why? They are not much bigger but 2 ½ times the cost. The singleton fit better in the duffle bag and the girls – still have not outgrown sleeping together in it at 18 months. The extra-bassinet is a waste for twins – because if yours are like ours – they will want to sleep together.
- **Pack-**N-Play Sheets – The mattresses are a little thin so you will want the padded sheets. Note twins do go through about 1 ½ times that of a singleton not twice.

- **Shopping Cart Cover** – these are harder to find and you will want them as they grow older. They do have them for twins or 2 siblings.

- **Crib & Sheets** – We purchased double of everything. In the end one crib is empty because our daughters to this day prefer to sleep together. If they are not together they do not sleep and neither do we. Every baby is different so I would wait to double up until you know for sure what you need.

- **Breast Feeding (Boppy) Pillows** – We had one for twins and then later one for singletons. In hindsight a single one is better as they get older for them to learn to sit up and works well with two.

Tips & Tricks for Surviving the first 6 weeks
1. **Sleep Training**
   We were never big proponents of sleep training with our singletons. When the girls came along we learned the hard way that sleep training was a must. There were some days that we were lucky to get 30 minutes sleep a night because the girls were on different schedules. Once I got one fed and down the other would get up – ready to eat. After weeks of pure exhaustion with no family to help us in Mexico – I reached out to a friend who had

multiples in the US for advice. The best advice we ever received was to sleep train the girls.

How do you do it? Feed them together and put them to sleep together at the same time EVERY day. No deviations. Yes it is difficult with the various meetings with consulates to exit Mexico – but still worth it. It will take time at first because for us that meant me waking one baby to get them on the same schedule. Using a football hold method to feed them both simultaneously and/or propping one on my knee with a bottle while breastfeeding the other. Yes it seems like you are playing a game of Twister but you get used to it.

We put our girls down at 10 AM, 3 PM, and 9PM every day. It took about 2 weeks for them to adjust. They will cry and so will you at times but if you hold on – you will be so thankful once everyone has adjusted. We kept them on this schedule even when they were separated. To this day – at 17 months they still take a nap at the same times although they are shorter now. They go to bed with little to no fuss.

2. Traveling

Traveling with twins can be an adjustment. Many things come up that you don't think about with a singleton or over the years of traveling by yourself. First you need at least 2 adults to travel with twins. Why? Because there can only be one baby per adult per aisle from what we have been told by all the major airlines in Mexico and even the United States. This is in case there is an emergency there are enough oxygen masks for the adult and child. We also found out that there is an age limit on who can serve as an adult. Our son was only 14 when his sisters were born so he was not legally old enough to hold his sister on the plane. This created a lot of issues for us in trying to fly to the various appointments with the U.S. Embassy and to return home.

You will also want to leave earlier for the airport with twins. It takes longer to get them out of the car and you are trying to clear twice as many babies, breast milk or formula through security. Whether in the United States or Mexico we found you should arrive at least two hours early for the flight.

3. Appointment Systems

Many of the appointment systems for the U.S. consulate, doctors, and others go by date of birth. For some reason it really throws people off when the babies have the same date of birth and last name. We hit this issue with everything from printing out their airline tickets (getting 2 for the same daughter versus one for each) to doctor's appointments, to passport appointment, and so on. The shortcuts for these systems were not designed to deal with multiples. As a result you will want to plan a little extra time to reduce any confusion on the processors part that there are actually 2 little people with the same birthdate. Otherwise you may end up having to make multiple trips versus getting 2 appointments on the same day. For example, when we went for the Mexican Passports – the online system only scheduled time for 1 child versus both. We had to clarify our appointment with the front desk that the 2nd name was actually a 2nd baby with the same birth date – not a middle name. They were kind to grant 2 appointments but had they not been able to accommodate it would have meant another hour trip to the SRE to process the 2nd baby.

4. DNA Test

One thing we never considered is how the various blood transfusions and genetic screening procedures in our case would impact DNA testing. Nor did we think that being a multiple would have a significant impact either. Having multiples ended up being a big source of confusion and costs in additional DNA tests. Unfortunately from other IPs I have worked with and articles on this topic – this appears to be a common occurrence with trying to immigrate multiples. What most people do not know is even if twins are not identical it is not impossible for them to have more DNA in common when you use genetic screening processes to eliminate less desirable genetic anomalies like we did.

5. No Hands Free

Many parents will carry their baby in one hand and a bag of groceries, diaper bag or other item in the second hand. Or even use that extra hand to open a door, go up in an elevator, etc. When you have twins – you have one baby for each arm unless your partner is there to help. My husband had to return to the United States after the first month to care for our other children. What that meant is the everyday things you take for granted of doing with that free hand goes out the window.

Appendix D — Considerations for Same-sex Parents

Avoid using more than one egg donor/one sperm donor per pregnancy
Some clinics provide procedures where they can splice the genes of two fathers to impregnate a single egg. Although this is a great thing scientifically, you'll create problems for yourself when it comes to getting U.S. citizenship for your child.

Some clinics offer the option of creating embryos from different fathers and/or mothers to be carried by same surrogate. This can complicate matters in the hospital or when registering the birth certificates because you will not know who the actual biological parent is. It is better to use a separate surrogate for each because DNA testing in Mexico is expensive. If you make a paperwork mistake with respect to the parent, you may have difficulty getting U.S. citizenship.

Don't put both fathers/mothers on the birth certificate
In a few cases, the Registro Civil allowed both intended fathers to be placed on the birth certificate. These cases didn't end well. The IPs' home country, Spain, refused to grant travel papers, so they couldn't take their daughter home. We have heard of similar conflicts in other countries. It is best to do the step-parent adoption in your home country when it is complete. If you want two mothers or two fathers on the birth certificate, the best path is to use only one parent's name for the Mexican birth certificate and the U.S. citizenship process. After returning to the U.S., go through a step-parent adoption. This process results in the issuance of new birth certificates in the U.S.

Appendix E — Induced Lactation

If you are a fan of breastfeeding, you should check into induced lactation so that you can breastfeed your child (whether you are a woman or man). We were able to successfully induce lactation to breastfeed our babies.

Before moving ahead with induced lactation, consult a physician. We followed the Newman-Goldfarb Protocols, which are described at http://www.asklenore.info/b.../induced_lactation/biology.shtml. You'll find numerous sources of information online.

Once you've completed the procedure, you pump your breast every two hours (or at least eight to 10 times a day) for 10 to 15 minutes per side. During the night, pump twice. Between 1:00 and 5:00 AM, pump at least once because your body is more relaxed during that time. I found this to be helpful. I recommend a high-quality breast pump such as the Medela Pump-N-Style.

Breastfeeding is more of a marathon than a sprint, so it takes dedication. At first you will produce what appears to be only a few droplets of water. Eventually, however, the milk will start to flow. (It took me three weeks to see results.) The volume increases over time as you stimulate the breast. I was up to 32 ounces a day by the time they girls were delivered.

Remember it is important to discuss your options with your OB/GYN or delivery doctor on what is best for your particular situation.

Proof that breastfeeding your baby born via surrogacy or adoption is possible. The nurses took a picture because they had never seen that before.

46147856R00069

Made in the USA
Lexington, KY
24 October 2015